HUGH
MacLENNAN

CRITICAL VIEWS ON CANADIAN WRITERS

MICHAEL GNAROWSKI, *Series Editor*

Other titles in preparation

CRITICAL VIEWS ON CANADIAN WRITERS

HUGH MacLENNAN

Edited and with an Introduction by

PAUL GOETSCH

McGRAW-HILL RYERSON LIMITED
TORONTO • MONTREAL • NEW YORK • LONDON • SYDNEY
JOHANNESBURG • MEXICO • PANAMA • DÜSSELDORF • SINGAPORE
SÃO PAULO • KUALA LUMPUR • NEW DELHI

HUGH MacLENNAN

ISBN 0-07-077365-3 Hardcover
ISBN 0-07-077653-9 Softcover
Library of Congress Catalog Card Number 73-9237
Printed and bound in Canada
1 2 3 4 5 6 7 8 9 0   JD-73   2 1 0 9 8 7 6 5 4 3

to

Avanel McKinnis

CONTENTS

INTRODUCTION

Early in his career, Hugh MacLennan made it quite clear that he did not intend to limit his audience by writing "regional novels, scientifically correct with respect to their own background." Canadian novelists, he argued in 1946, should permit themselves only universal themes and compete on equal terms with American writers if they hope to find their "avenue to a world audience."[1] At the time, MacLennan's intention may have seemed over-ambitious; but it soon became evident that he was able to reach a world audience and yet resist the temptations of the popular novelist. He has neither, as Alec Lucas points out, repeated his successes in "any obviously intentional way,"[2] nor followed the fashions set by American best sellers. Rather, he has continued to dramatize contemporary problems within a Canadian setting and to analyze them thoughtfully. It is therefore no small achievement that his books, which after all contain many elements of a peculiarly Canadian nature, have travelled so well. *Two Solitudes*, for instance, went into eight languages, and, by 1970, *The Watch that Ends the Night* had been translated into Spanish, Swedish and German, and had sold 700,000 copies in Canada and the United States and an additional 150,000 copies in England.

In spite of the measure of popularity MacLennan enjoys in Canada and abroad, the critical reputation which he has gradually built up for himself in Canada has hardly crossed the southern border and the Atlantic. He is, for example, still little known in literary circles in my own country, Germany, where his novels have done particularly well, with the sales of *Barometer Rising* and *The Watch that Ends the Night* standing, in 1970, at 70,000 and 220,000 copies respectively. Apart from the condescending stance which German literary critics like to take with regard to authors adopted by leading book clubs, one may surmise that the critical climate here is not favourable to a writer who does not belong to the avant-garde and who, at first sight (and, to some extent, even on closer inspection), tries to do for Canada what American novelists did for the United States some time ago. At any rate, in Germany and, I suspect, outside Canada in general, Hugh MacLennan has yet to be acknowledged by critics as a writer who wrestles with contemporary problems of universal, not only Canadian, concern.

On the other hand it would be wrong to expect that he can ever be as highly esteemed abroad as in Canada. It is, I think, not unfair to say that, judged in international terms, he is at best a good minor postmodernist writer though he is a novelist of major importance for Canada and the history of Canadian fiction. On the whole his Canadian critics have been aware of this. While it is true that some reviewers have tended to laud enthusiastically whatever MacLennan chose to do, the majority of critics have time and again voiced reservations—especially against his unashamed didacticism, the obtrusive nationalism of his first books, his self-conscious treatment of emotions, and his conservative techniques. The case against MacLennan has been most cogently presented by Robert H. Cockburn,[3] but even from his book MacLennan emerges as a novelist who is important for Canada in many ways. Most critics would, it seems, agree with George Woodcock's cautious evaluation:

> Hugh MacLennan occupies a position of uneasy eminence in Canadian letters. He is probably the most considerable novelist our country has yet produced, yet this is a statement one can make only to the accompaniment of elaborate qualifications.[4]

Despite such qualifications, however, Hugh MacLennan has fared fairly well at the hands of his Canadian critics. They have dealt competently with the major aspects of his fiction. Understandably enough they have paid special attention to his attempt to assess the nature and development of Canadian society.

As is well-known, MacLennan felt at the beginning of his career that it was necessary to make "literary maps" of his country and provide "literary archetypes" for it if he wanted to explain Canada to herself and the rest of the world.[5] By 1954 he had come to believe that he no longer needed to worry so much about the problem of unfamiliarity. "The goal of the Canadian writer today," he concluded, "is therefore much the same as that which confronts his brother writers in France and England: how to produce a work of art, a work possessing international value, in the late maturity of an established tradition of art and writing."[6] This insight marked a change in his approach to national problems but not in the nature of his self-appointed role as "Canada's secretary."[7] After *The Precipice* he continued to deal with important Canadian issues though in a less self-conscious fashion. As he himself said of *The Watch that Ends the Night*, ". . . the author at least felt as free in his Canadian milieu as any American or Englishman in his."[8]

The importance and ambitiousness of MacLennan's themes are undisputed. But, as critics were quick to notice, his intentions as a social realist involved him in problems of form. In 1949 Robert Weaver echoed many reviewers when he maintained that MacLennan's main characters "sacrifice their reality as individuals under the load of social comment and analysis which they are required to support."[9] This charge was soon taken up by Desmond Pacey, R.E. Watters and the early George Woodcock, and has indeed become a commonplace of MacLennan criticism. With Hugo McPherson's succinct analysis of "the problem of Hugh MacLennan's art," the question of form began, however, to be seen from a slightly different perspective. McPherson justified the contrived plot and the typical characters of *Barometer Rising* and argued: "The symbolic structure which worked well in the treatment of social conflict stumbles over the concealed trip-wire of individual uniqueness in the later novels."[10] He thus pointed to a shift of emphasis in MacLennan's works and indicated that the novelist is not a social realist pure and simple but a writer who uses symbolically contrived plots successfully. This suggestion has been influential. As I myself argued in 1961, MacLennan owes much to the romance, with its air of probability in the midst of improbability and its proximity to mythic and allegoric forms of order, when he tries to describe the movement from catastrophe to a quiet affirmation. Recently, Alec Lucas devoted one chapter of his brief study on MacLennan to "Uses of Romance" and another to "Types and Myth," without denying that MacLennan's fiction has "many of the qualities of a social documentary."[11]

If McPherson's essay has made it possible to appreciate MacLennan's formal departures from social realism proper, George Woodcock's essay, "A Nation's Odyssey," has encouraged critics to look more closely at those symbolic and mythic patterns in which the novelist's vision crystallizes. What, according to Woodcock, distinguishes the rather old-fashioned novels is MacLennan's use of the Odysseus myth:

> . . . the *Odyssey* itself was the product of a people in the process of becoming aware of itself and, appropriately, the theme which MacLennan uses it to illuminate is the growth of a Canadian national consciousness.[12]

In his valuable, though too short, booklet of 1969 Woodcock has substantiated this argument by referring to MacLennan's essays and discussing the classicist bent of the writer's mind. Despite MacLennan's own mild disclaimer,[13] Woodcock's thesis has gained wide, if not general, acceptance. Douglas Spettigue has, for instance, put it to good use to explain *Return of the Sphinx* in terms of the end of the heroic quest. The case of the dissenters has been most strongly argued by Robert Cockburn, who cannot discover any symbolic characters outside *Barometer Rising* and attributes the recurrence of character types rather to a poverty of imagination on MacLennan's part than to any intricate masterplan. Alec Lucas, too, has mounted an attack on "A Nation's Odyssey," but his suggestion that other Greek myths are of greater importance for MacLennan than Odysseus' wanderings, does not invalidate Woodcock's general approach. Woodcock himself has, by the way, pointed to correspondences between *Return of the Sphinx* and the legend of Oedipus, as have Peter Buitenhuis and others.

As several recent studies have proved, MacLennan's novels sustain a rigorous analysis of their imagery and their archetypal patterns. D. G. Jones and Warren Tallman have placed some of MacLennan's key images in the wider context of Canadian literature; William H. New and Kathleen O'Donnell have commented on the functions of the imagery and the setting; and Dorothy Farmiloe has illuminated Jerome Martell's flight from the lumber camp with reference to MacLennan's own remarks about the Canadian voyageurs and to the initiation *out of* society characteristic of Mark Twain's Huckleberry Finn (a point also made by Peter Buitenhuis and Tom Marshall). There still seems to be room, however, for a systematic study of MacLennan's settings and their symbolic import, for his use of geography "helps to define his personal myth of Canada."[14] Such a study should discuss, among other things, his handling of pastoral motifs, his view of the city-nature antithesis, and the functions which his love of the land serves in the novels.

Though for some years critics have concentrated on patterns of myth and imagery, MacLennan's role as an interpreter of the Canadian social and political scene has not been neglected, least of all, of course, by George Woodcock himself. Increasingly, critics have used MacLennan's essays to expound his views on history and Canadian problems (for instance, Paul Goetsch, R. H. Cockburn, George Woodcock).

One of the topics still worth investigating is the question of how MacLennan's interpretation of Canadian history and society relates to that of Canadian historians and public opinion makers. MacLennan, I suggest, has often been the spokesman for the Canadian Establishment, and not always to the advantage of his art. *Barometer Rising*, for example, takes up one cliché dear to Canadian historians and politicians and asserts, rather than dramatizes, Canada's role as "the golden hinge," as a mediator between the United States and the United Kingdom. Another cliché enters into *The Precipice* when MacLennan describes the relationship between Canada and the United States in terms of a good wife helping her robust but worried husband. As a study of the image of the United States in Canadian fiction would reveal, the idea that America needs the spiritual support of Canada is not uncommon. It is not MacLennan's use of stock notions as such which is disturbing. The trouble is that they often remain clichés in his novels and thus force the reader to share Edmund Wilson's impression:

> . . . one feels that in his earnest and ambitious attempt to
> cover his large self-assignment he sometimes embarks upon
> themes which he believes to be socially important but which
> do not really much excite his imagination.[15]

Another area of investigation is suggested by Robert D. Chambers' "Hugh MacLennan, a Canadian Novelist." Taking MacLennan's essay, "Roman History and Today," as a point of departure, he ascribes to the novelist a powerfully dramatic view of history and then proceeds to assess the importance of the conflict of generations in Mac-Lennan's fiction. This kind of approach may yield still more pertinent results if carried a step further. Not only in "Roman History and Today" but also in his Ph.D. thesis and in a number of early articles on his intentions and his situation as a Canadian writer, MacLennan has discussed the question of cultural decadence and renewal and has described the movement of history in terms of successive cultural cycles. As he argues in "Roman History and Today," there are tides in the affairs of men that no individual can possibly stem. This is particularly the case whenever the ideas and causes of a given order have become too remote. It is only when a new era, a new cycle, begins that a man is free enough to change these causes and thus determine the fate of his society. Such opinions may help to explain MacLennan's interest in the phenomenon of social change and the conflict of generations. They also reveal, however, why Canada—its birth as a nation *(Barometer Rising)*, its awakening from its Victorian sleep *(The Precipice)*, and its escape from the problems of the Thirties *(The Watch that Ends the Night)*—became a suitable subject matter for him. To the young classicist and historian, a breakthrough in a different direction seemed necessary in the 1930s, but he doubted whether this was possible, for "the mainstream of Western culture" had become "a deep layer of soft mud from which the clean spring water" had "poured away." When turning to Canada, the younger member of the "American branch cycle,"[16] he apparently began to feel more optimistic and came to believe that there perhaps even the novelist might contribute a little to the future.

If his ideas on the general movement of history are indeed the rationale, or, at least, one of the major reasons, for his original interest in his own nation, it is obvious why only important issues of Canadian society would do for him as *exempla* showing the way to a general cultural renewal and reconstruction. It is equally obvious why in *The Precipice* Canadians as members of the younger nation are able to serve as spiritual guides to Americans, or why Mac-Lennan did not remain satisfied with the first part of *Two Solitudes* but felt obliged to go on and suggest a solution to the problem of national division. Less obvious is perhaps the fact that MacLennan's view of history is not altogether at odds with that sense of destiny hovering over his novels which several critics have explained by both his Calvinist background and his classicist training (for instance, George Woodcock and Peter Buitenhuis).

I do not wish to argue that the cyclical view of history which emerges from MacLennan's early nonfiction is the key to all of his novels. If there is such a key at all, it is rather to be found in his belief that ours is an age of both social and spiritual crisis. In his first novels he seems to assume that, at least in a young, vital nation like Canada, man's spiritual needs may be stilled by a trust in the future development of the country. In his later novels he has come to trust less in society and to rely more on the consolations which private experiences of a religious nature afford. In other words, he has recognized—most poignantly so in *Return of the Sphinx*— that Canada enjoys no special status within the American branch cycle of culture. Therefore he is now more concerned with private than social solutions to the question of how life can be affirmed in the face of modern scepticism, materialism, violence and chaos.

This does not mean, as left-wing critics asserted after the publication of *The Watch that Ends the Night*,[17] that MacLennan has turned his back on society, now denies the possibility of coherent positive social actions, and seeks refuge in personal love. As Alec Lucas observes,

> MacLennan is no more opposed to rational than to social action (although the anti-intellectualism of much of the modern movement dismays him). It is only that he believes neither can succeed unless motivated by or based on the same elements that help constitute personal love; namely, tolerance, kindness, compassion and benevolence—all qualities that have little place in a purely rational ethic.[18]

In *Each Man's Son*, *The Watch that Ends the Night* and *Return of the Sphinx* MacLennan has continued to show how history and society intersect the private lives of his characters, but the social world is, in a sense, no longer his major concern; it serves chiefly as the stage for the personal drama.

How MacLennan's religious views have developed and how much they owe to his private quarrel with his Calvinist background has been described by a number of critics. Roy Daniells talks of Mac-

Lennan's fiction as religious allegory based on Calvinism, Peter Buitenhuis compares *Each Man's Son* to Hawthorne's analysis of Puritanism, and, with Hugo McPherson and others, has emphasized the contrast between *The Precipice* and *Each Man's Son* to illuminate the writer's deepening interest in psychological and personal problems. It may still be rewarding, however, to relate the novels to MacLennan's essays on religious questions, to discuss in detail his view of the conflict between Puritan repression and the instinctual life, and to examine the religious imagery he uses in *The Watch that Ends the Night*.

Whether he is "essentially a religious novelist"[19] or not, his novels are expressions of his search for values. They take many of the experiences and problems incorporated in the modern novel for granted but then move on to search for a positive solution. In dramatizing his search for values and affirmation, MacLennan has, like other postmodernists, fallen back on older techniques of novel writing. Critics have therefore been at pains to relate him to the British,[20] the American,[21] or the Canadian tradition.[22] Interesting as some of their comparisons may be, they run the risk of making MacLennan appear an old-fashioned writer and, thus, of denying or obscuring his contemporaneity.

It is the purpose of this collection to document the major trends in MacLennan criticism and to suggest that MacLennan's reputation so far rests chiefly on *Barometer Rising* and *The Watch that Ends the Night*, though some critics (for instance, George Woodcock and R. H. Cockburn) have expressed a preference for *Each Man's Son*. For reasons indicated above, the bulk of this volume consists of contributions by Canadian critics. There are a number of studies I should have liked to include, in particular, Woodcock's "A Nation's Odyssey," Edmund Wilson's idiosyncratic discussion of MacLennan, and the introductions to *Barometer Rising* and *Each Man's Son* by Hugh McPherson and Alec Lucas, respectively. But for reasons of space I had to decide against reprinting essays and passages from books still in print. This accounts, too, for the omission of recent discussions of MacLennan as an essayist.

The University of Freiburg   PAUL GOETSCH
1 March 1972

NOTES

1. MacLennan, "Canada Between Covers," *Saturday Review of Literature,* 29 (Sep. 7, 1946), pp. 28 and 6.

2. Alec Lucas, *Hugh MacLennan* (Toronto, 1970), p. 2. Cf. *ibid.,* pp. 2-3 for a survey of the sales of MacLennan's books.

3. Cf. the bibliography at the end of this volume for detailed references to this and others critics mentioned in the introduction.

4. G. Woodcock, *Hugh MacLennan* (Toronto, 1966), p. 1.

5. MacLennan in a letter to the present writer (Oct. 6, 1959).

6. MacLennan, "Writing in Canada—Its Position Today," *Royal Military College of Canada Review* (1954), p. 130.

7. E. Wilson, *O Canada: An American's Notes on Canadian Culture* (New York, 1966), p. 68.

8. See note 5.

9. R. Weaver, "A Sociological Approach to Canadian Fiction," *Here and Now,* 1 (June, 1949), p. 15.

10. H. McPherson, "The Novels of Hugh MacLennan," *Queen's Quarterly,* 60 (1953), p. 187.

11. Lucas, *op. cit.,* p. 57.

12. G. Woodcock, "A Nation's Odyssey," in *Masks of Fiction,* ed. A. J. M. Smith (Toronto, 1961), p. 129.

13. Cf. MacLennan, "Postscript on Odysseus," *Canadian Literature,* no. 13 (Summer, 1962), pp. 86-87.

14. T. Marshall, "Some Working Notes on *The Watch that Ends the Night,"* *Quarry,* 17 (Winter, 1968), p. 13.

15. Wilson, *op. cit.,* p. 68. Cf. my German dissertation for a study of how MacLennan's views relate to the tradition of literary nationalism in Canadian criticism.

16. MacLennan, "Canada Between Covers," p. 6. For a brief comparison between MacLennan and Toynbee see S. Lynn, "A Canadian Writer and the Modern World," *Marxist Quarterly,* 1 (Spring, 1962), p. 38.

17. Cf. the essays by A. Roberts and S. Lynn. For a similar view cf. Hirano's essay in this volume.

18. Lucas, *op. cit.,* p. 56.

19. *Ibid.,* p. 57.

20. See, for instance, the writings of George Woodcock.

21. Cf. my essay in *Canadian Literature* and the book by P. Buitenhuis.

22. See, for instance, W. H. Magee, D. G. Jones, W. Tallman.

HUGH MACLENNAN

GEORGE WOODCOCK

To a critic whose thoughts on fiction have been based principally on European and American novels, perhaps the most striking thing about Hugh MacLennan's three books is the extent to which the various aspects of Canadian nationalism—or perhaps rather of the growth of a Canadian national consciousness—form an imposed pattern within which the lives of the characters are worked out. The psychological development which most European nations underwent in the half-century round about 1848, which reached its height in the United States during the era after the Civil War, and which has since weakened in such countries (at least as a major motive in imaginative writing), is still strong in Canada. I do not propose here to criticize MacLennan because he seems to have become intellectually dominated by this sense of cultural nationalism. Clearly, Canada has been undergoing a certain historical development which is perhaps inevitable, and it is only natural that this development should find its expression in the literary art of the country. Nevertheless, it is a factor which must be taken into account in any attempt to analyze the nature of a novelist's work and motives; it even, I think, bears a close relationship to the most perceptible weaknesses of MacLennan's work.

Barometer Rising, MacLennan's first novel, is his least elaborately contrived; it is also, in my opinion, the best integrated of his novels, and one of the few recent books of Canadian fiction that really hold their own with the better novels being published today in England and the United States.

The setting is Halifax during the First World War, and the central situation is somewhat self-consciously worked out. A young man returns secretly to the Nova Scotian capital with the intention of righting a wrong he has suffered; it transpires that he is an officer whom his uncle, also the colonel of his battalion, had attempted

"Hugh MacLennan," by George Woodcock. In *Northern Review*, 3 (April-May, 1950), pp. 2-10. By permission of the author.

to blame for the failure of an attack in France. By chance the young man, Neil Macrae, is bombed on the night before his court martial, and given up for dead; he is, however, found and patched up without his real identity being discovered, and he returns home, risking execution for cowardice and desertion, in the hope of getting the evidence to clear his name. Meanwhile, there still lives in Halifax the cousin, Penelope Wain, with whom he was in love before he went to the war; she, besides being a capable ship designer, is the daughter of his enemy.

Wain and Penelope both learn of Macrae's presence in Halifax, and, while the Colonel sets out to frustrate Neil's efforts and to get rid of him with as little trouble as possible, Penelope and a drunken M.O., the proverbially raffish "good egg," do their best to see that Macrae succeeds in vindicating himself. But the efforts of both parties reach a climax, not through their own powers, but by the inhuman intervention of the great Halifax explosion, which overshadows the latter part of the novel. Macrae and Murray, the drunken doctor, recover their self-respect by superhuman feats of endurance to relieve the victims of the catastrophe, while Colonel Wain is providentially one of the corpses removed from the ruins, and Neil happily acquires the evidence that proves his innocence.

Barometer Rising is a satisfying novel. The atmosphere, the very physical feeling of Halifax three decades ago, are well evoked, and the action moves with the right sense of momentum to the great climax of the explosion. This is represented in a really powerful passage of descriptive reporting which gives a most vivid expression of a catastrophic event:

> When the shock struck the earth, the rigid ironstone and granite base of Halifax peninsula rocked and reverberated, pavements split and houses swayed as the earth trembled. Sixty miles away in the town of Truro, windows broke, and glass fell to the ground, tinkling in the stillness of the streets. But the ironstone was solid, and when the shock had passed it resumed its immobility.
>
> The pressure of the exploding chemicals smashed against the town with the rigidity and force of driving steel. Solid

and unbreathable, the forced wall of air struck against Fort
Needham and Richmond Bluff and shaved them clean,
smashed with one gigantic blow the North End of Halifax
and destroyed it, telescoping houses or lifting them from
their foundations, snapping trees and lamp-posts, and twist-
ing iron rails into writhing, metal snakes; breaking buildings
and sweeping the fragments of their wreckage for hundreds
of yards in its course. It advanced two miles southward,
shattering every flimsy house in its path, and within thirty
seconds encountered the long, shield-like slope of the Citadel
which rose before it . . . .

Underneath the keel of the "Mont Blanc" the water opened and the harbour bottom was deepened twenty feet along
the channel of the Narrowa. And then the displaced waters
began to drive outward, rising against the town and lifting
ships and wreckage over the sides of the docks. It boiled over
the shores and climbed the hill as far as the third cross-street,
carrying with it the wreckage of small boats, fragments of
fish, and somewhere, lost in thousands of tons of hissing
brine, the bodies of men. The wave moved in a gigantic bore
down the stream to the sea, rolling some ships under and
lifting others high on its crest, while anchor-chains cracked
like guns as the violent thrust snapped them . . . .

But long before this, the explosion had become manifest
in new forms over Halifax. More than two thousand tons of
red-hot steel, splintered fragments of the "Mont Blanc," fell
like meteors from the sky into which they had been hurled
a few seconds before . . . .

Over the North End of Halifax, immediately after the passage of the first pressure, the tormented air was laced with
tongues of flame which roared and exploded out of the atmosphere, lashing downwards like a myriad blowtorches as
millions of cubic feet of gas took fire and exploded. The atmosphere went white-hot. It grew mottled, then fell to the
streets like a crimson curtain. Almost before the last fragments of steel had ceased to fall, the wreckage of the wood-
en houses in the North End had begun to burn. And if there
were any ruins that failed to ignite from falling flames, they

began to burn from the fires in their own stoves, onto which they had collapsed.

Over this part of the town, rising in the shape of a typhoon from the Narrows and extending five miles into the sky, was poised a cloud formed by the exhausted gases. It hung still for many minutes, white, glossy as an ermine's back, serenely aloof. It cast its shadow over twenty miles of forest land behind Bedford Basin.

The chapters describing the rescue work, which succeed this passage, are maintained at a level of vigorous action, and the diminuendo from catastrophe to the saddened realization of human happiness makes just the appropriate final touch to the balance of the novel.

A number of literary threads can be seen woven into the texture of *Barometer Rising*, and, in general, they continue to appear in the later novels. To a different scene, and in the language of a different age, there is applied a technique of building up local atmosphere very similar to that used by English novelists with a regional interest, like Hardy and Bennett. Indeed, the influence of more modern writers on MacLennan seems to be, at most, superficial, and, in his values as well as in his conception of fictional form, he appears to belong rather to that conception of "classical" novel writing whose heyday in England ended with the Georgians. The characters and their attributes have changed and are brought into line with their different backgrounds, the devices of modern reportage have been appropriated to give an apparent, though often fallacious realism; but in the elaborately contrived plot, in the tendency to divide characters arbitrarily into the blacks and whites, the undoubted villains like Colonel Wain, the excellent girls like Penelope, the essentially sound men pushed a bit off the rails by misfortune, like Macrae and Murray, *Barometer Rising* is the kind of novel which would probably show little life of its own and little significance in a wider sense if it were written within an older literary tradition. As it is, the application of more or less traditional attitudes and techniques to a new environment and historical situation, give them new life and make *Barometer Rising*, despite its lack of experimental interest, a remarkably fresh and stimulating book to read.

Another feature MacLennan shares with some of the older novelists, and particularly Hardy, is the fact that his own education in antique classicism has left its mark. There is a reminiscence of the Greek tragedians in the way the young man, returning like an avenger, is able to witness the just (in a tragic sense) destruction of the man who has sinned, not so much against humanity as, through his overweening ambition, against the Gods. And MacLennan provides the clue to a Homeric influence when he gives his heroine the name of Penelope and makes her lover say, after her faith and patience have been rewarded in the unexpected return of the man thought dead: "Wise Penelope! That's what Odysseus said to his wife when he got home. I don't think he ever told her he loved her. He probably knew the words would sound too small."

It is perhaps due to the author's classical background that the action of *Barometer Rising* has a certain mechanical momentum which at times takes the action out of the hands of its characters. Beyond a certain point, they no longer shape their own fates, but become the puppets of external events, and it is not so much through the relationships and efforts of people that the plot is finally worked out, as through the apparent accident of the explosion, which seems to take on life and become a kind of superhuman influence, dealing out death to the good and evil with an undiscriminating hand, but inexorably preparing the fulfilment of the elect. It is at this point that the classical influence seems to unite with the Calvinist philosophy of Nova Scotian religion.

A final, and rather badly managed influence to be detected in *Barometer Rising* is that of the mystery story. The first chapter, in which the hero is introduced, gives the picture of a young man with a mission without telling the reader his identity; in the same way, it is some time after she is introduced that we learn the full story of Penelope's early relationship with Neil Macrae. In neither case is the withholding of information essential to the plot of the book, since the actual process of the struggle between the characters provides suspense enough, and a rather hollow air of mystification is thus given at the outset to a novel which does not need it.

Yet, despite these criticisms, I think *Barometer Rising* remains the most completely satisfying of MacLennan's novels, and, in its way, one of the most interesting examples of recent Canadian fiction.

Barometer Rising is linked with MacLennan's novels, not only by common influences and techniques, but also by the preoccupation of its most significant characters with the destiny of Canada. At times this almost destroys the fictional pattern. For example towards the end of the book, when Neil and Penelope are leaving the devastated city, there comes this paragraph of soliloquy on Neil's part, protruding like a jagged spur among the warmly personal thoughts which one would expect to dominate two young people united at last after many vicissitudes:

> He looked down the car and saw the lines of quiet bodies sway gently with the train's motion. Why was he glad to be back? It was so much more than a man could ever put into words. It was more than the idea that he was young enough to see a great country move into its destiny. It was what he felt inside himself, as a Canadian who had lived both in the United States and England. Canada at present was called a nation only because a few laws had been passed and a railway line sent from one coast to the other. In returning home he knew that he was doing more than coming back to familiar surroundings. For better or worse he was entering the future, he was identifying himself with the still-hidden forces which were doomed to shape humanity as certainly as the tiny states of Europe had shaped the past. Canada was still hesitant, was still ham-strung by men with the mentality of Geoffrey Wain. But if there were enough Canadians like himself, half-American and half-English, then the day was inevitable when the halves would join and his country would become the central arch which united the new order.

Here, in an unassimilated and crude form, is made evident that idea of the growing unity and identity of Canada which dominates MacLennan's later books. Such a blatant and abstract statement of the problem carries no kind of fictional conviction, and it is fortunate that in *Barometer Rising* such passages are short enough not to detract materially from the human feelings and fears and relationships which are the necessary substance of the novel.

In *Two Solitudes* the idea of Canadian unity becomes the main symbolic theme, which MacLennan here attempts to work out in a concrete manner through the lives of his characters. Not unnaturally, he tackles that relationship, between French and English Canadians, in which the problem of unity appears farthest from solution. The action begins in the little Quebec village of Saint Marc, which is dominated partly by Father Beaubien, and partly by the seigneur, Athanase Tallard. Tallard is a politician with anti-clerical leanings, who would like to see the material progress of Western Canada introduced among his fellow French Canadians. The latent conflict between him and the extremely anti-English priest only becomes evident when Tallard is the means, first of introducing a Protestant farmer into the village and then of interesting a group of English Canadian financiers in the possibilities of industrial development which the village offers. This struggle is complicated by the landlord's personal relationship with his elder son, a French Canadian nationalist who is arrested as a deserter during the 1914-1918 war, and who helps to arouse hostility against his father. Eventually, goaded by the priest's obstinacy, Tallard renounces his Catholicism. He is boycotted by his neighbours and, worse than this, his English industrial partners desert him when they see that his unpopularity will harm their material interests. Bankrupt and worn out with anxiety, he dies in Montreal, returning to the church and being accepted again by his neighbours when he is taken back for burial in their midst.

This part of *Two Solitudes* could easily form a complete novel, and it evokes very sensitively the atmosphere of French Canadian village life and the character of the English-speaking financial rulers of Montreal. Not only are Tallard and his prejudiced but sincere enemy, Father Beaubien, very deftly drawn, but there are equally good portraits of Tallard's sensual Irish wife, of his second son, Paul, and of the Nova Scotian Protestant settler, Captain Yardley, a man of natural and humane wisdom whose instinctive tact earns the grudging respect of his Catholic neighbours. Yardley, indeed, is the centre of some of the most sympathetic passages of the novel. Here, for instance, is part of the account of a fishing expedition, showing how adroitly MacLennan can at times work his central theme into the fabric of his incidents. Yardley, his two granddaughters and Paul are the characters who figure in the incident.

They moved into deep water with no sound but the creaking of the oar and an occasional splash as it broke water. The bow nodded gently back and forth as the sculling oar propelled them onward. When they came to a shoal where a stake was driven into the riverbed Paul moored the boat and they cast their lines. By sunrise Paul and Heather had caught two fish apiece and the captain had four. Daphne had not taken any, though she had lost two.

While they fished, the sun rose. It rolled like a ball out of the river and its rays shot through the mist like red arrows. The ball mounted and paled to gold, shredding the clouds apart. Paul thought it was like the candles over the altar, gleaming on the cloth-of-gold chasuble of the priest at Mass, the cry going up to the roof and the suggestion that this golden light was the colour of glory. The mist stirred and lifted in veils. Flashes of light struck out from the church steeple in the village. Farther upstream there was a similar gleam from the steeple of Sainte-Justine, and across the river another. Then the aluminum paint on the church roofs began to shine; the world was bright and it was day. In all the parishes up and down the river the angelus rang. The notes had a muted, rolling sound as they came over the water. Paul bowed his head and Daphne looked at him oddly. He kept his head bowed as he murmured a prayer to himself, and Daphne finally glanced at Heather with a smile that was half embarrassed and half amused. The captain frowned at her.

When the angelus ceased ringing Daphne said, "Do you always do that? "

"Yes. When I'm awake. It's for the angelus."

"It's a funny thing to do."

"That's rude," Yardley said. "Talking about other people's religions."

"But I just think it's funny Paul being a Catholic that's all."

"Catholics think it's a hell of a lot worse, us being Protestants."

"Mummy says you shouldn't say hell," Daphne said.

Yardley eyed her reflectively. "Listen, young lady—some day I'm going to tan you."

This first part of *Two Solitudes* has a very close unity, bound together by the common anxieties of the war and the close identity of the larger problems of the racial conflict with the actual daily lives and relationships of the characters. The problem here seems to grow from the story, rather than, as in the strictly didactic novel, the story being fabricated around the problem. If *Two Solitudes* had ended with Tallard's death, it would certainly have been Mac-Lennan's most impressive and moving book. But he was not content merely to state his problem in terms of concrete reality, and in the second half of the book moves forward to the statement of an arbitrary solution. Paul Tallard, the second son of Athanase, who becomes a merchant seaman, meets again and eventually marries his childhood friend, Heather. Here, clearly, is symbolized the end of racial divisions. And in the process, as always happens when an intellectual concept begins to take precedence in a novel, the characters become depersonalized and unconvincing. In Paul's struggles there is nothing so solid and moving as in his father's defeat, precisely because the latter moved in a concrete pattern of living and in a predominantly human environment where personal relationships, and not intellectual abstractions from them, were the prime moving factors. Moreover, there is an air of contrivance about this latter part of *Two Solitudes*; it is only because Paul has been fortunate enough to receive an English as well as a French education that he can make the necessary connection, first of all within himself; and his own personal solution, therefore, does not represent a true symbol even of the wider social situation.

The Precipice, MacLennan's most recent novel, is in many respects a parallel work with *Two Solitudes*. It also is dominated by a rather generalized view of the Canadian scene, in which an Ontario small town, with all its faults and virtues, is shown in opposition to the American urban way of living, the "precipice" of New York. A young woman of the Canadian town, caught in the interests of a petty and narrow-minded community and apparently destined to a perpetual spinsterhood in a house of sisters, suddenly becomes involved in a relationship with an American businessman, whom she marries and who takes her to New York. Here, after many trials, the marriage breaks up, and shortly afterwards the husband's business affairs crash, his nerve breaks, and the family is re-united in a "slick" happy ending which, if it does nothing else, at least shocks the reader into astonishment that a writer capable of good work can write at times so banally.

The Precipice is, indeed, an extremely disappointing book, beginning well but declining steadily into mediocrity. The early chapters, describing the lives of the three sisters, in their circumscribed non-conformist background, are really stimulating and lead one to expect a good novel. But already, in the rather cheap devices by which the meeting of Lucy and Lassiter, her American lover, is contrived, there is a foretaste of the later development, and the book slowly disintegrates into a typical sentimental romance of the too-good-to-be-true wife who loyally supports her husband in an environment which she hates and who, after he has betrayed their marriage, nobly forgives all and consoles him in his downfall.

Once again, as in *Two Solitudes,* the validity of the early part of *The Precipice* is negated by the rest of the novel. The small town atmosphere is real, the artificial life of New York fails to convince, so that the contrast intended by the author is never sufficiently impressive. Moreover, while the characters begin as real personalities, they later merge into puppets working out a formularized plot and intellectual concepts. Lucy Cameron becomes a smug and irritating paragon, her husband a comic caricature of the advertisement agent, while the mechanical working out of events, already a perceptible fault in earlier novels, here becomes almost completely dominant.

Hugh MacLennan has, I think, all the essential gifts of a good novelist, without ever having written a really satisfying novel. At his best, he can develop character very capably, he has an excellent sense of locality and a great power of description. His writing has so far been impeded, not so much by any intrinsic literary faults, as by a tendency to submit to motives which are extra-literary. He attempts to make his work illustrate an intellectual pattern, he tries to write in order to convince a hypothetical public of the truth of certain vague social concepts. He does not yet seem to have realized that such concepts will only appear true in fiction when they emerge from writing instead of being imposed on it, when they arise naturally from the interaction of personalities and the organic development of situations and relationships. Such a restriction of writing within limits which have no literary validity is bound to cramp its possibilities of development and eventually, as in *The Precipice,* to destroy not only the novel itself, but even the lesson it is intended to illustrate.

THE NOVELS OF HUGH MACLENNAN

HUGO MCPHERSON

Hugh MacLennan's novels have survived both a domestic enthusiasm and the criticism of the larger world of English letters. Bernard de Voto is "a profound admirer of the novels of Hugh MacLennan"; J. Donald Adams (of the *New York Times*) considers Hugh Mac-Lennan "your best living novelist." The great popularity of the Czech translation of *Two Solitudes* affords an international comment upon MacLennan's broad appeal. Popular criticism, however, has concerned itself largely with MacLennan's handling of such problems as Puritanism and Canadian nationalism; it has tended to ignore his technique, and its relation to his increasingly complex themes.

Barometer Rising and *Two Solitudes*, the first novels, have an almost classical clarity and simplicity of structure. Each, on multiple levels, deals with the theme of self-realization or rebirth; in each, the personal conflict is significant finally as an image of a larger, symbolic conflict of social forces or attitudes. By objectifying social forces in real, though *typical* characters, MacLennan creates a dramatic and realistic story whose meaning, in Melville's phrase, "rays out" as from a lighthouse, beyond the individual to the national or even the universal.

But in *The Precipice* and *Each Man's Son*, novels which examine the *psychical* as well as the social problems created by Puritanism, the allegorical or "typical" technique breaks down. It becomes clear in these novels that the technique of symbolic characterization is not, without radical alteration, adequate for the representation of characters who are at once symbolic figures and unique psychological case studies. This is not, of course, to argue that a symbolic character cannot also be uniquely individual. The artist's

"The Novels of Hugh MacLennan," by Hugo McPherson. In *Queen's Quarterly*, 60 (Summer, 1953), pp. 186-98. By permission of the author.

problem is to find a means or *form* which makes possible a simultaneous representation of *both* the symbolic and the unique.

The problem of Hugh MacLennan's art, then, is formal. The symbolic structure which worked well in the treatment of social conflict stumbles over the concealed trip-wire of individual uniqueness in the later novels. The increasingly complex nature of MacLennan's artistic vision has not been fully supported by parallel developments in technique. The resulting dilemma will be examined in detail.

*   *   *

Barometer Rising (1941) is MacLennan's best-constructed allegory. Superficially, it is a simple tale. Neil Macrae, a falsely discredited army officer, returns to Halifax in 1917 to accomplish two things: vengeance upon his uncle, Colonel Wain, the author of his disgrace; and reunion with his sweetheart, Penny, the Colonel's daughter. At the moment when Neil's vengeance becomes possible, the city is blasted by the explosion of a munitions ship. Colonel Wain is killed. In the nightmare of rescue work which follows the disaster, Neil and Angus Murray (a second suitor of Penny's) regain the self-reliance of which the war has robbed them. Neil and Penny, with their illegitimate child, are ready to begin a new life.

Neil's story is a rebirth pattern. The dynamic behind his desire to be revenged on Colonel Wain is a long-standing rebelliousness against the family and the social group in which he had grown up. Sent to Europe, disgraced in battle and robbed of vengeance by the explosion, he is led to re-examine and realign old values. He emerges from the cataclysm a mature man, possessing a new awareness of Canada's status and of his own place within the national corpus. Like Edgar in *King Lear* (Neil remains incognito until after the disaster), or Theseus retracing the labyrinth, Neil is an archetypal figure. His wound, his supposed "death," his return and vindication are, in microcosm, the record of youthful Canada, betrayed into war but returning home with a new knowledge of its own identity.

Throughout, the literal and the symbolic levels of the story are firmly controlled and fused by the omniscient point of view which

Mr. MacLennan employs. In general, the narrative method combines the stream of consciousness with a cinematic technique. The author may begin a scene within the mind of one of his characters, quickly focus upon the immediate scene and then, with the smoothness of a mobile camera, withdraw to a panorama in which the characters disappear from view. So consistently is the image of the city and harbour maintained throughout the story that Halifax and its society assume a character equal in force, and parallel, to that of Colonel Wain. As the carefully ordered time sequence (*Sunday, December 2, to Monday, December 10, 1917*) slowly unrolls, the reader sees Halifax with the freshness of first-hand vision. At the moment of the catastrophe, while the city hangs on the sickening edge of disaster, it becomes clear that images such as that of Colonel Wain in the arms of his mistress represent the smug self-indulgence of Halifax—of the "old" Canadian society. The organic relation between the microcosm of the plot and the macrocosm of social conflict thus stands revealed.

The skill with which MacLennan makes his full symbolic meaning explode upon the reader at the exact moment of the physical explosion which climaxes the story is the greatest technical achievement of the book. Neil Macrae, we know, represents an army coming home in the bitter belief that war is a cheat and peace a mask used in high places to disguise ambition and the profit motive. Similarly, Colonel Wain, the general who is fascist in all but name, symbolizes a reactionary social group; he is the archetype of the tyrant father.

On the evening of December fifth, in Halifax, two forces of retribution are poised for action: Neil Macrae on the individual level, and the materials of war (a munitions ship) on the economic-social level. Through his own ambitious self-seeking, Colonel Wain has betrayed his nephew; through its own callous self-seeking, its blind wish for war profits to keep on accumulating, the society of Halifax (or Canada) has betrayed its younger generation into the pain and horror of war. Both have sown the seeds of sin: both are about to reap the whirlwind of death and disaster. In Hugh MacLennan's hands, then, the Halifax explosion is made to illustrate an individual, social and even mythical pattern.

In the last section of the book (during the rescue work, with the cheering knowledge of the courage of the average citizen manifesting itself on every hand) Neil realizes that he "has changed too much to care for . . . [the revenge] he had a right to enjoy." In losing this obsession (the bitterness of the homecoming army, the disillusion of the adolescent in society) he experiences an epiphany—he suddenly "sees into" his personal life and gains the initiative to act confidently upon that understanding. Thus he speaks, too, for the nation which now knows that the catastrophe of Halifax is not the same as the tragedy of Europe—which knows that Canada is a young country able to supersede the "old" and establish its own pattern.

Such a summary account of *Barometer Rising* ignores several flaws. Perhaps the most serious flaw is the intrusion of two or three baldly didactic statements of the social-national theme. They weaken the structure because (like the moral of an *exemplum*) they have already been better stated dramatically. The important thing is that, formally, the novel is more justly proportioned and more suggestive than any preceding Canadian novel.

* * *

Barometer Rising owes its success in large part to the clearly delineated social framework within which its characters move. It gives expression not only to the conflicts of individuals and social groups, but also to a basic, archetypal pattern. Unlike John Steinbeck, with his often inept and muddled analogizing in *The Grapes of Wrath*, Mr. MacLennan has maintained a precise and exciting equivalence between his superficial action and his larger theme or themes.

In *Two Solitudes* (1945) this equivalence is again established and maintained. The structure which supports its personal themes of self-realization is a thesis-antithesis-synthesis pattern. Like the warring Titans, Captain Yardley and Athanase Tallard fail in their quest; but Paul Tallard and Heather Methuen, the second generation, achieve (symbolically) a synthesis.

Unlike *Barometer Rising, Two Solitudes* emphasizes the conflict of social groups. Each of the major characters symbolizes one aspect of this knotty social problem in a direct, one-to-one ratio: Marius is the French Canadian nationalist; Janet is the British imperialist; Huntly McQueen is the thrifty, Scottish Calvinist; Father Beaubien is the chauvinistic Roman Catholic; Athanase Tallard and Captain Yardley are the French and English Canadians who try to share in both cultures; Kathleen Tallard is the Irish Catholic misfit. Among the young people, Daphne is the Canadian who attempts to forget the problem in an artificial cosmopolitanism; Paul and Heather are the French and English young people who, when cosmopolitanized, will fuse the diverse elements of Canadian society into a new and mature Canadianism.

The story is constructed in triad form: root position, the background of the French-English social struggle, focused upon Athanase Tallard and Captain Yardley, the men of good will who fail equally in their attempts to heal the schism in Canadian life; second position, the meeting and separation of Heather and Paul who, still tied by parochial attitudes, cannot establish a common meeting ground between French and English; third position, a "return" of the now mature Heather and Paul culminating in a marriage symbolic of the union of opposed forces in Canada.

The symmetry of this plan equals that of *Barometer Rising*. Unfortunately, the inversions of the triad strike with diminishing force. Like Nathaniel Hawthorne in *The Marble Faun*, Mr. MacLennan became fascinated with the first demand of his theme, the establishing of the necessary background. Moreover, the career of Athanase Tallard, who dissipated his potential powers of statesmanship in loving too many women, proved to be worthy of a full-length novel in itself. After devoting 218 pages to Tallard and the struggle of the older generation, the author diminished the execution of Parts II and III to near-skeletal form. These sections (152 pages) have about them a forced and tentative air: they are thin in characterization; they are withered by arid narrative. Where the problems of the first section are bodied forth in the dramatically ingratiating actions of Captain Yardley and the erratic flourishes of Athanase Tallard, the problems of intellectual-emotional growth treated in sections II and III too often present themselves in set-piece dialogues or long passages of baldly prosaic thought. Characters who were important, symbolically, in I, are later dismissed casually; thus Kathleen, the Irish Catholic misfit, loses her symbolic identity by retiring to the arms of an American businessman; Father Beaubien, now facing the major problem of a factory in his ancient parish, is silenced by an unexplained bishop's edict.

The story deteriorates dangerously when Paul Tallard's years of emancipation abroad are summarized in a few pages and Heather's years in cosmopolitan New York are condensed into a few letters. The literal-symbolic parallel almost disappears at one point, when a "poor-boy, rich-girl" tension, rather than a conflict of racial backgrounds, appears to be the cause of Paul and Heather's separation. The final chapters rally as the triumph of the new culture, symbolized by the marriage of Paul and Heather, is presented to imperialist Janet as a *fait accompli.* Even this excellent scene, however, cannot compensate for a resolution that is largely verbal and theoretical.

The flaw of *Two Solitudes* is not merely thinness of execution. It is a failure to discover an adequate "objective correlative" for the presentation of intellectual development. Twice in *Barometer Rising* Neil fell into didactic, unrealistic (and unnecessary) reverie. The "objective correlatives" of the "explosion" and rescue work had *already* expressed dramatically his inner conflict and its resolution. In the last parts of *Two Solitudes* this dramatic "objective correlative" of the subjective situation is largely lacking; thought has vaulted beyond flesh into abstraction. This practice of "telling about" important or even crucial mental events becomes more serious in *The Precipice* where self-conscious reverie and set-piece dialogue abound. The form of the early novels thus proves inadequate to the author's new *psychical* materials.

Of *The Precipice* (1948) Mr. MacLennan said: "Actually what I was trying to do was to find a common denominator between U.S. and Canadian tradition which I believe exists in the Puritan background of both countries." *The Precipice*, that is, *attempts* to analyze the various psychological manifestations of Puritanism and to reveal the impact of Puritanism on North American social behaviour.

Clearly, this is a thematic innovation for Hugh MacLennan; it forces him to treat social problems and, simultaneously, to go *inside* the consciousness of his protagonists in order to work out dramatically the genesis of particular Puritan inhibitions. Even more clearly, such a theme demands a new kind of structure. In presenting mental events, the author must find either a parallel to the "explosion" of *Barometer Rising*, or a completely new technique which will by-pass stagey dialogue and "told about" reverie. In *The Precipice* no solution is vouchsafed; the symbolic "type" and "unique individual" remain unreconciled.

The formal problem encountered in *The Precipice* deserves illustration. The first section of the novel uses the symbolic technique of *Two Solitudes*; the primary significance of the characters is rooted in, or rises out of, a generalized problem. Because the author's integrity will not allow him to present his problem in the gross contrasts of black and white, he creates a group of characters who represent many shades and tints of the Puritan dye: Jane Cameron, the austere, traditional Calvinist; Bruce Fraser, the Promethean intellectual rebelling against Calvinism; Lucy Cameron, the heroine, Bruce's female counterpart; Stephen Lassiter, the hero, American youth attempting to lose Puritanism in economic success; Carl Bratian, the American immigrant turned pragmatist.

The first section of the book is convincing and provocative. It develops most of the symbolic characterizations: Jane, dominating her sisters with blind, Calvinist conviction; Lucy, analyzing but failing to free herself from the repressions of the Puritan community; Stephen, apparently capitalizing upon his own peculiar heritage of New England Calvinism, and so forth. But once the action moves away from the circumscribed, definable community of Grenville, Ontario, the most serious difficulties arise. In exact parallel to the failure of *Two Solitudes* to dramatize the "cosmopolitanizing" effect upon Heather and Paul of New York, Oxford and Athens, *The Precipice* fails to illustrate the "de-Puritanizing" effect of New York, England and Princeton upon Stephen, Lucy and Bruce.

The difficulty, of course, is simply that "New York" and "England" resist *definition* too strongly to be used as symbols of a "de-Puritanizing" force. Moreover, with the exception of minor characters like Carl Bratian, no non-Puritan forces are really created.

Instead, the symbolic figures are led out into the real world where, as symbols on any level, they no longer function. The symbolic technique has broken down.

On the level of psychological representation there is a related failure. To begin with, the large number of characters required to illustrate various "sets " of the Puritan attitude makes the psychoanalytical task a vast one. The technique of "literal summary of mental life" places the author in the position of a lifeguard trying to save a dozen drowning people. To present the full personality-complex of eight or ten characters would require much more space than four hundred pages. On the other hand, to eliminate a study of any one of the characters would falsify the theme by making it appear more black or white and less grey. Lacking a new solution to this problem, the author attempts to analyze almost all of his persons. The result is an essential and pervasive thinness of characterization. Even Stephen and Lucy, who are treated in some detail, are more often summarized than *presented*.

The formal problem raised by the author's new interest in psychological action should now be clear. Arbitrary descriptions of mental events, or prosaic, unobjectified streams of consciousness, fall short of MacLennan's needs; a new approach to structure is called for. Formally, *The Precipice*, despite the depth and challenge of its theme, is a failure.

* * *

Each Man's Son (1951) reveals Hugh MacLennan's consciousness of the formal weaknesses of *The Precipice*. It is an attempt to move beyond the allegorical structure of *Barometer Rising* to a full-length portrait of a single individual surrounded by characters who, define his society and objectify the forces at work within his personality. For Daniel Ainslie, Puritanism is a personal problem which, however confusedly, he works out for himself. His ultimate "escape" to England is, perhaps, MacLennan's admission that the Puritan problem cannot be solved in the social-symbolic manner of *Two Solitudes*.

The theme, the "ancient curse" of Calvinist austerity, is explicitly stated in a Prologue. The background is a Scottish mining community on Cape Breton Island. Daniel Ainslie is a brilliant mine doctor whose need to give and receive love (to find a benevolent rather than a repressive faith) forces him to deny the God of Calvin and to seek an acceptable object for the great warmth which he feels within himself. Driven by this consuming need, he centers his affection upon Alan MacNeil, the son of a simple-minded prize fighter who is vainly attempting to establish a reputation in the United States. When Alan's mother finally wrests her son from Ainslie's benevolently possessive grasp, the doctor is desolated. In an introspective passage, ending in an epiphany that the reader does not quite understand, (again one feels the lack of an "objective correlative") Ainslie's disillusion sets him free from the "ancient curse." But soon, as an indirect result of the doctor's possessive love for Alan, violent death overtakes Mollie and Archie MacNeil. Ainslie takes charge of the orphaned Alan and, a "father" at last, he "escapes" from Cape Breton's narrowness to the emancipated world of England where his scientific talent can develop freely.

Though this synopsis seems simple the story is filled with persons and incidents whose exact significance is puzzling. On the one hand, some of the characters are blurred relatives of the types of *Two Solitudes*: Louis Camire, the admirer of Mollie MacNeil, is an alien "socialist"; Mrs. MacCuish is a spectral arch-Calvinist; Mrs. Ainslie represents softened New England Calvinism. On the other hand, some of the characters seem significant as *psychological* symbols (a new and important structural innovation): Mollie and Mrs. Ainslie are both mother figures specifically related to Ainslie's memories of his own mother; Alan MacNeil is associated with Ainslie's boyhood; Dr. MacKenzie, the founder of the hospital, is a father image—the man Ainslie might like to resemble or replace.

Other suggestions of a larger dimension of meaning tantalize and thwart the reader. The individual miners become comments upon the narrowness and futility of the Calvinist community; their daily descent into the bowels of the earth is linked, perhaps, with the Calvinist conception of man's depraved nature. Similarly, Archie MacNeil, who rejects "going down into the pits" for a life of "prize fighting," seems to represent the unregenerate lost in a Godless world (the U.S.A.). Dr. Ainslie's sterilization of his wife, his denial of Mollie's maternal rights and his scorn of his mother's supposed weakness, all carry with them the sense of a sexual maladjustment springing from more complex roots than the simple Calvinist fear of sensuality. The whole Promethean pattern of Dr. Ainslie's conflict (his need to defy the God image, his need and inability to become a father himself, his desire to devote his talent to the good of mankind) suggests a psychological and even mythical meaning which transcends and invalidates the over-simple thesis of the "ancient curse."

But despite this wealth of suggestive character and incident, no clear light "rays out" beyond the surface gloss of *Each Man's Son.* A resonant, coherent *form* for the representation of mental conflict is still lacking. Moreover, the departure from "type characterization" and tight, symbolic structure has not, in this novel, marked the accession of a structure which keeps physical action and stated theme in consistent, organic relation. In the closing chapters, for example, we learn that Dr. Ainslie has, obscurely, won his spiritual battle by conquering his "son" obsession. But Mollie, perhaps through fear of losing her son, has accepted the amorous advances of Louis Camire. Archie MacNeil, arriving home, broken and disillusioned, discovers his wife in the arms of her lover. In the ensuing battle, witnessed by little Alan, both Mollie and Camire are killed. Archie dies of a blood clot on the brain. As a result of this violent homecoming, Dr. Ainslie is left to look after the young orphan whom he has so long loved.

Such dramatic elimination of all the obstacles to Dr. Ainslie's wishes provides an effectively startling *dénouement.* However, the relation of this speedy nemesis of three characters to the theme of the "ancient curse" is not clear. If, on the psychological level, these three deaths represented a symbolic exorcism of the traumatic forces at work in Dr. Ainslie's personality, they would be relevant; but there is no ambiguity (such as we find, for example, in the tragic events of Henry James's *The Author of Beltraffio* or *The Turn of the Screw*) suggestive of a psychological or symbolic dimension in the MacNeils' tragedy.

Each Man's Son, in relation to the body of Hugh MacLennan's fiction, must be considered as experimental and transitional. Without abandoning completely the form of the early novels, it reaches out a tentative, exploratory hand towards new forms and new ideas. One need only consider the widely contrasted works of Virginia Woolf and Franz Kafka to visualize the diverse areas which Mr. MacLennan is now attempting to synthesize. The magnitude of his undertaking commands our respect and admiration.

HUGH MacLENNAN, A CANADIAN NOVELIST
HERMANN BOESCHENSTEIN

I

The Canadian Hugh MacLennan has recently published his fifth novel: *The Watch that Ends the Night* (1959). The work was an immediate success on the bookstands. Though high sales are no proof of its true worth it does show the interest that MacLennan has stirred up in Canada and the United States. He has received several literary awards and there are grounds for hoping for truly outstanding achievements. His creative power is as indefatigable as Morley Callaghan's and his talent even more diverse. He commands an unusual versatility of style, offers the reader a profusion of motifs, events, thoughts and new techniques, and he carries out the trade of the narrator with passion. He has first-hand knowledge of working people, yet he is a man of education and learning. MacLennan studied classical history and is currently teaching English Literature at McGill University in Montreal. He is as at home in contemporary intellectual movements as he is familiar with the wide ranges of modern psychology. Nor does he shrink from sharp criticism of the Canadian situation. Roy Daniells calls him "the most provocative of our novelists."[1]

Nevertheless, the latest novel is still not the long-awaited masterpiece. It does not fulfil the expectations of his first novel, *Barometer Rising* (1941), but it does show that he has more than one arrow in his quiver. One feels that his development will take time and labour and one readily extends him credit.

MacLennan's novels have long suffered from the demanding tasks he imposes upon his literary figures, but especially from his compulsion to sketch the typical, ideal Canadian and bring him to life in a novel.

"Hugh MacLennan, ein kanadischer Romancier," by Hermann Boeschenstein. In *Zeitschrift für Anglistik und Amerikanistik*, 8(1960), pp. 117-35. Translated by C. Maurice Taylor. By permission of the author and the publisher.

Barometer Rising can be considered the great attempt at portraying the awakening self-awareness of Canadians and their national and cultural character. This is achieved symbolically through the course of events and theoretically through the historical and cultural-political observations. The explosion which wrecked and burned the city of Halifax in 1917 is presented as a true event and simultaneously as a highly symbolic event: the past is destroyed, the war has stretched its fearful hand even to far-off Canada, but Canada will recover in a different way from Europe and go on to develop into a great spiritual force. The terrible accident caused by the collision of two munition ships solves the personal problems of Neil Macrae, the returning soldier; but the reader willingly accepts this intervention of fate because it exposes, literally and figuratively, the forces which will make possible the rebuilding of the city and Canada's progress towards becoming a civilized nation. Colonel Geoffrey Wain, who tried to send his nephew Neil to his death, to avoid giving him his daughter Penny in marriage, lies buried in the rubble. Nothing stands in the way of the marriage. In Wain we see the death of the colonial Canadian, who would like to lease his country both culturally and economically to England. In Neil we see the new, independent Canada striding towards a better future.

At the same time there is a familiar note struck in the novel, as though age-old myths and tales were being told. Hugo McPherson who wrote the foreword to the reprint of the novel points out that *Barometer Rising* traces again that fairy-tale path through life where a jealous old man sends a young hothead on a dangerous and, he hopes, fatal adventure.[2] The youth escapes his destiny, returns as the shining hero, settles accounts with his enemy and wins both kingdom and daughter. The ancient plot is clearly woven into the novel with no chance that the writer's contemporaries will ever forget the message. Once Neil has recognized that his lucky escape from war and the explosion can only be accounted for through belief in the future of his homeland, he becomes and remains the embodiment of the national spirit. The only criticism of this patriotic view is that it never has the opportunity to prove itself in the novel through deeds. Neil remains rational even in moments of great emotion. He studied engineering in Boston before the war and respects Americans just as he later learned to esteem Englishmen. He wants nothing but what world history—as he sees it—seems to demand: Europe tore itself to pieces between 1914 and 1918 and abrogated its role of guarantor of prosperity and progress. Canada must take over the leading role. Good as that may be for every Canadian, it still places a burden of responsibility upon his shoulders. He must be forgiven a mixture of pure, almost childlike pride in living in a country whose physical greatness is on par with its economic and cultural possibilities. The feeling that overcomes a Canadian, when his thoughts take flight across his country and he sees oceans off each coast with green fields and woods in between, the blue of the inland lakes, the golden wheatfields of the west and the obelisks of the Rocky Mountains, has often been described. Along with joy and gratitude he is moved to make a solemn oath to collaborate in the opening up of this thinly settled land and to help with the spiritual awakening of this giant body. An exclamation such as this comes straight from the heart:

> . . . this anomalous land, this sprawling waste of timber and rock and water where the only living sounds were the foot- falls of animals or the fantastic laughter of a loon . . . this beadlike string of crude towns and cities tied by nothing but railway tracks, this nation undiscovered by the rest of the world and unknown to itself, these people neither American nor English, nor even sure what they wanted to be, this un- born mightiness, this question mark, this future for himself, and for God knew how many millions of mankind! [3]

A military doctor, Major Murray, an American by birth and a Cana- dian by choice, helps to put into words the future role of Canada when he speaks of Canada's role of arbitrator between England and the United States. It will cease to be a mere colony, without quite becoming a completely independent country. He foresees that Eng- land and America will be thrown back on one another more and more. Canada must not rush headlong into the arms of either nation. It must remain free for the task of building "the keystone to hold the world together." This is somewhat presumptuous. Mur- ray has to take some of it back and reproach himself for an overly artificial plan. On the other hand, Neil in his enthusiasm is to be allowed to give himself without restraint to the certainty of the rebirth of his homeland. Why not? Canadians like to abandon themselves to such dreams, which certainly must have been much livelier after the First World War than they are today. In those days hopes were not fixed so exclusively on the stock market and production curves but rather spun out romantically, in the direction of the Far North. André Siegfried sees the North as the lodestone that sets the mystic soul of the otherwise sober Canadian vibrating.[4] Neil is not the kind of romantic who combines a search for adventure with a search for gold. He wants Canada to have a spiritual awakening and become a civilized nation. At one point, deeply struck by the change, he said, in effect, "A few years ago we thought we were a nation because we had promulgated a few laws on the subject, and had laid iron rails from east to west, but to-day we feel the nation growing from within and acquiring a soul and spirit." We can pardon him, if on occasion he is so brash as to proclaim that from now on Canada must direct the fate of mankind, determined up to now by small European states; he is simply overcome by unhoped-for lover's bliss and reaches for the most exalted tasks in order to bear it. He is, for all that, no blatant nationalist. There is a unique, subtle tone to Canadian national consciousness and the pioneer spirit of strong independence and peaceful teamwork is part and parcel of it. No Canadian—this time generalization is not out of place—ever thought of shaking a clenched fist at the future while looking around for an enemy on whom to vent his anger.

Whereas in archetypal stories the hero returns from dangerous exploits, marries and leads a long and happy life, Neil has to merit his bliss by doing something great or at least by resolving to do something great. MacLennan lays down his pen only when both have been assured: the double happiness of love and the prospect of a life filled with effective action. Under the impression that the writer is describing his own transformation in Neil's awakening and in the certainty that he will continue on his chosen path and make good his patriotic promise, the reader reaches in anticipation for his next work.

II

Two Solitudes (1945), MacLennan's second novel, immediately returns to the national theme. One is tempted to assume that he will avoid at all costs the excessive youthful exuberance of *Barometer Rising*. The many and varied difficulties of a national rebirth, that Neil overlooked as a returning soldier, now come to the fore. The old historical forces weigh like lead over the vision of the future. The past has not vanished from the earth as in Halifax; its strong presence is still felt, dividing Canadians as it always has into Englishmen, Frenchmen, Catholics and Protestants. To bring forth the model Canadian of tomorrow, Canadians of today with their dissensions and differences must first be fused together. But they fight against it and cling to the very things that separate them. Is this the true situation? The critics accused the writer of exaggeration, although, or perhaps because, he sees *Two Solitudes* as a clear reflection of reality and therefore a genuine novel of Canada. MacLennan points out that there is still no adequate word to describe a Canadian. When French Canadians speak of "Canadien" they are referring to themselves. The others are "les Anglais." English Canadians on the other hand refer to themselves as "Canadians", and the others as "French Canadians", so that it is left to each group to determine the meaning and scope of the narrow term.

The writer would agree, I am sure, that, his characters are too stereotyped. He sets the action where the drastic and tragic outcome is, if not inevitable, at least possible. Montreal by necessity represents the stronghold of English Canadian big-business and the east bank of the St. Lawrence the heart of French Canadian bitterness. The period in which the story begins takes care of the "crises." It is 1917; the federal Government has finally decided to introduce conscription. Quebec is on the verge of insurrection for, if need be, young French Canadians are to be dragged from their beds at night and hauled off to the barracks.

French and English Canada are the two solitudes that the famous Rilke expression alludes to. Neither side makes an effort to refute the accusations which have been raised. The Anglo-Saxons are as bored, arrogant and materialistic as the Quebeckers assume they are. The Quebeckers on the other hand are the perfect picture of backward *habitants* as seen by English Canadians. The opposing elements are not even at peace in one individual who represents both sides. Athanase Tallard, who leaves the most lasting impression, owns the seigneury in the parish of Saint-Marc; he belongs to one of the oldest families, his ancestors having come to Canada from France in 1672. As a member of the Lower House he represents the rights of his French Canadian brothers without being a parish-pump politician. He has friends far and wide, and under favourable circumstances such connections would be bound to create a splendid type of man, and a fruitful life. In the unfortunate circumstances of the times, however, what results is a divided being who finds respect and favour with neither French nor English, nor even a comfortable living.

Tallard's life is soon torn apart by his two marriages. His first wife was the exemplary French Canadian woman of the soil, pious, a pillar of the Church, unworldly, almost a saint. She enhanced the Tallard name in the same degree that his second wife, of English background, young and full of life, destroyed it. A son was born of each marriage. Marius, the first-born, inherited his mother's hatred of English Canadians. He is, as MacLennan says, the mathematical product of the conflict raging within the country and within the Tallard family. He does not get along with his stepmother. He preaches against conscription and thereby alienates himself from his father who nevertheless tries to protect him when the police arrive to take the dissenter away. Paul, the son of the second marriage, possesses his father's talent for reconciliation. He will, as shall be shown, continue in his striving to become a well-integrated Canadian.

Tallard, the father, is crushed between two millstones, a victim of the grossest misunderstanding and complete lack of forebearance from both the French and the English. MacLennan's Quebec reflects nothing of the cheerful, idyllic world conjured up by Victor Hémon in *Maria Chapdelaine*. The few good-natured *habitants* who appear now and then in Drouin's General Store to pick up their mail and exchange the latest news are too much under the influence of the village curé to be able to keep their common sense and courage in a crisis. Beaubien, the Catholic curé, dominates his flock just as the Church dominates the village setting—it is, we hear, larger than the largest Protestant church in Montreal. Beaubien feeds the still vigorous, centuries-old hatred of English Canadians, whose fathers invaded the peaceful homes of French Canadians and destroyed *La Nouvelle France*. Nor is France any better, says the priest. It abandoned the settlers along the St. Lawrence, murdered its own anointed king and sold itself to the devil of godlessness. There is nothing left for Quebec but to be what it has always been, a place of refuge in the chaos of the times. Let it poison peace with new discoveries and the mad scramble for money. Quebec will be mindful of God and its immortal soul. It is the Church's aim in life to keep the fires of remembrance burning brightly.

Such views are not uncommon in Quebec and one often hears about Quebec fanaticism. MacLennan describes what many have seen, by introducing a priest who is as dogmatic in his religion as he is provincial in his politics. We first meet Beaubien stepping out of the presbytery to stretch his legs and get a breath of air. He paces briskly back and forth, one hand on his pendant cross with his black soutane swishing along the ground. He is the picture of energy with his stride, his nose, his wide, straight mouth. His eyes look magnified behind his thick glasses. This is the man who will not be cowed by Tallard, the absolute master and beneficiary of an old tollbridge. The battle between the two begins when Tallard is about to sell a parcel of land with a waterfall on it to an English Canadian finance group in Montreal. The priest cannot stop the power plant and the advent of industry but he does ruin the middleman, the traitor to Quebec's time-honoured traditions. Despised by his neighbours, Tallard is forced to move to Montreal only to learn that he is not respected there either. He has become a burden to industrialists and stockholders alike. They have found a better helper in the person of the bishop, who has been convinced that a factory would provide employment for many young men, good Catholics who would otherwise have to move away. Tallard must endure the final insult of being labelled a prototype of the backward French Canadian. Although he had the best intentions and only wanted his habitants to follow modern economics and science without losing the freedom of their way of life, he fell victim to both French Canadians and English Canadians. He wore himself out in the search for a reality that does not yet exist: harmony between the two racial halves, and mutual progress.

In order to underscore the incompatibility of the two solitudes, MacLennan brings another English Canadian to Saint-Marc, the former Captain Yardley, who buys a farm. Whether or not he really is the first English Canadian to succeed in buying a farm in Quebec, he nevertheless moves away some years later, happy to return to his native Nova Scotia, where he plans on spending his declining years in peace. Quebec cannot tolerate even this good-humoured and wise outsider.

With the same sharply etched lines MacLennan sketches the English Canadian opponents of Beaubien and his flock: the business and upper-class people of Montreal. Only a few peripheral figures from the English Canadian world win our sympathy. Besides the previously mentioned Captain Yardley, there is the major who returns from the First World War and stops in Montreal for some amorous adventure. He is a counterpart to Neil Macrae in *Barometer Rising*, except that he is much less absorbed in the expectation of national rebirth; the only mention of it is interwoven in the erotic episode with none other than Tallard's second wife. The major is angry at all the foreign embellishments disfiguring Canada.

> . . . Canada isn't England, and too many Canadians try to
> pretend it is. Generally they're the rich ones, and they pay
> the money and make the choices. Does our western prairie
> look like anything in England, for God's sake? Then why try
> to cover it with English architecture? . . . After a while they'll
> get another idea. They'll pretend we're exactly the same as
> the States. And they'll start to imitate ideas from down
> there. But is there anything in the States like the Saint Law-
> rence valley? For that matter, is there anything in the States
> like us—the collective us?[5]

This is a very homespun kind of national pride. It may lack depth, but at least it is an upright and honest one that looks to the future, and better than what MacLennan says about the upper-class Montrealers. The leading English Canadian circles are, as has been suggested, no better in their way than the sheep and shepherd of Saint-Marc. Although the eccentric traits of the French Canadian have long had their place in English Canadian literature, the English Canadian businessman has never been sharply drawn. Here MacLennan had to break new ground and rely upon his own observations for his characterization. He seems to have drawn upon a living model, one who for many Canadians has become the symbol of an era, thank heavens, now long past: the former Prime Minister of Canada, William Lyon Mackenzie King (1874-1950).

* * *

In *Two Solitudes* the role representing English Canada falls mainly to financier Huntly McQueen. Is the name an obvious camouflage for King? One is inclined to think so since MacLennan wrote about Mackenzie King several times. The man, to whom Canadians entrusted their political fate for many years, surely embodies in purest form the essence of his voters and represents the typical English Canadian of his time. MacLennan has not only thoroughly discussed Bruce Hutchison's book on Mackenzie King, *The Incredible Canadian*,[6] he also placed Mackenzie King at the beginning and end of an essay on the Canadian national character.[7] McQueen is presented as simultaneously cautious and irresponsible in much the same way that MacLennan presents Mackenzie King as a fierce watchdog that somehow manages to look both good-tempered and somewhat melancholy. Even the personal characteristics of McQueen are like the prime minister's. Mackenzie King, as we read in the article, lacked flair and imagination. He did not care if he gave the impression of indecisiveness because he could pursue his aims all the more stubbornly under that guise. Boring, an awkward bachelor with the soporific voice of a preacher, Mackenzie King nevertheless exercised a strong will underneath his considerable frame. It would appear that only a man of such duplicity and cunning could keep the two halves of Canada together during the stressful periods of two world wars. For this reason MacLennan can portray him as one of the few political geniuses that Canada has produced.

McQueen resembles Mackenzie King, and traits of both men are to be found throughout the English Canadian business world. Its single-minded goal, says MacLennan, is to create, achieve, and spread prosperity—spread could even mean no more than passing on an occasional tip on the stock market to a good friend. The English Canadian masters show their worst side when they run up against the opposition of young people who are interested in intellectual and artistic things, rather than the stock market. For McQueen, too, the hour is fast approaching when he must bend the will of such distasteful people to his own way of thinking. He learns that the daughter of English Canadian friends would like to marry Tallard's second son, Paul. With his double prejudice against French Canadian blood and idealistic youth he feels obliged to prevent this misalliance. But he arrives too late; the young couple have already married and are resolved to lead a life of protest against English Canadian plutocracy.

MacLennan is thereby able to continue the elder Tallard's attempt at uniting the two racial halves in his son. Paul, however, has been better prepared. He knows the ordinary man; he had to struggle through university; during the Depression he went to sea, then on to Oxford with his savings and finally settled in Athens to write the novel that weighed on his mind: *Young Man of 1933*; an important title, for MacLennan uses it to announce a new theme to which he will devote a good measure of his strength. The years between 1930 and 1939 have definitively formed him and his generation. Economic crisis, the "Fata Morgana" of ideologies, and above all the terrible reality of goose-stepping fascists, profoundly disturb him. Paul Tallard, believing he can break through this nightmare, burns his manuscript on his honeymoon. In such a state of bliss he wants to write about something better than the feckless youth of the day. First, however, there is the Second World War to get through. He volunteers and we may reasonably expect him to return in 1945, fate allowing, with the same nationalistic hopes that Neil Macrea felt in Halifax in 1917. In his later novels, MacLennan will again touch upon the national theme and return over and over to the patriotic sparks that jump when a Canadian becomes acquainted with Europe. He does not however, develop it to any great depth nor even enter into a lively discussion of it.

III

Two Solitudes is the all too clear parable of the two halves of Canada that refuse to grow together. In *The Precipice* (1948), MacLennan's third novel, the same didactic aims are clearly visible throughout. This time the Scottish Calvinists and American Puritans become the target of his remarks. From the very outset we are told that it will take some hundred years before Calvinism's influence on Canada is likely to disappear. What is the significance of this pessimistic forecast? The Scots are stringent with themselves and relentless in their judgments of other people. In carrying out their duties they are fanatics. Duty for them means hard work, rigid orthodoxy and regular church attendance. At the same time they dismiss humour and art, frivolity and fancy as dangerous temptations. The source of MacLennan's scorn and censure is the town of Grenville. Any Canadian would automatically substitute the correct geographical name of Belleville, Ontario, for Grenville, without disputing the fact that Bellevilles are found all over Canada.

> Here was lodged the hard core of Canadian matter-of-factness, on which men of imagination had been breaking themselves for years.
> Grenville was sound, it was dull, it was loyal, it was competent—and oh, God, it was so Canadian![8]

Nevertheless MacLennan's satire does not reach the proportions of a large-scale attack such as the Canadian Seldwyla deserves. He shows the harm caused by the icy wind of Calvinism and its potential control, but in his sense of justice he also shows the moral energy that Presbyterianism can and does exert at times. The yarn out of which the threads of the plot are spun, is in the hands of the three Cameron sisters, the orphan daughters of a minister. Although they inherited little real money, they do hold a substantial Presbyterian mortgage. In the course of time the sternness of the older daughter, Jane, softens to a dependable kindness; the youngest, Nina, is lost to the attractions of the big city; Lucy, the middle daughter, marries an ambitious American businessman. She makes the best use of her Presbyterian talent by saving her husband from moral and professional ruin through her fidelity and spirit of self-sacrifice. We hardly need point out that marriage between a Canadian and an American is a ready-made occasion for elaborating on national differences.

Besides the above characters, there are others who consciously disassociate themselves from the Scottish moralizers. Bruce Fraser, the son of a good Presbyterian doctor goes to Montreal, ostensibly to study "the liberal arts," but above all to taste the splendidly immoral life of the city. He notes that Canada is much more than the Province of Ontario with its Scottish sobriety, lack of emotion and the constant struggle to suppress every movement of the heart. With Neil and Paul, Bruce is now the third member of the league who wants to lead Canada into an independent future. Like Neil in the First World War, he discovers in the Second World War the spiritual and cultural possibilities of his homeland Once again the patriotic visionary waves his magic wand, but MacLennan does not bring the treasures to light.

Matt McCunn fights against Grenville in a different way. While still a minister he announced from the pulpit his battle against the joyless faith of his fathers, subsequently resigned his ministry and struggled through somehow, with the help of the bottle and a good sense of humour. The Second World War enables him to make a virtue out of his negative feelings towards the bourgeois way of life and his own lack of business sense. He becomes an excellent sailor and a brave soldier, almost a hero. When he lands in Dubrovnik bringing supplies to the Partisans, and once again finds himself near the same Germans he fought against in the First World War, he is overcome, for perhaps the first time in his life, with a touch of homesickness for Grenville. The incident is more important than he realizes. What draws McCunn back to Grenville and makes the Presbyterian citizens endurable in spite of everything is the Celtic-Gaelic streak in him that hasn't quite vanished. The rigidity of his faith has not completely destroyed the lust for life inherited from his Gaelic ancestors.

One must realize that MacLennan—with his Scottish Highland background—considers the part played by the Highlanders in the development of Canada of prime importance. They made their Canadian home in Cape Breton, the island off the coast of Nova Scotia. Countless Highlanders have settled there since 1820, forming a closed ethnic and linguistic group, matched only by that in Newfoundland. Gaelic was long spoken there and only in recent years has it given way to English. Ancient customs still thrive there; legends and tales from Celtic times are still spun along with the wool, and are often embroidered with stories the men bring home from the sea. There are still farmers on Cape Breton who take to the sea in search of fish or sign up on a ship when farming proves unproductive. Coal-mining has been carried out on Cape Breton for hundreds of years. The struggle for existence is hard, but the people cling to their traditional feasts and fun all the more tenaciously.

Time and again in his essays, MacLennan has defended the view that the Highlanders of Cape Breton are, after the English and the French, the third prominent racial group to give a unique, unmistakable stamp to Canadian history.[9] Elsewhere in his writings he has honoured the contributions of Germans, Dutch, Italians, Icelanders and Ukrainians.[10] It is no surprise that he felt compelled to build a literary monument to the imaginative, tuneful people of Cape Breton.

IV

Each Man's Son (1951) is for the greater part a regional novel about the Gaelic world of Cape Breton with its characteristic serenity and attendant hardships. As Pastor McCunn realized in *The Precipice,* the devil of an evil conscience nips at the heels of the good-natured Highlanders. In the preface to *Each Man's Son,* we read that they have brought with them the curse of a religion that forces them to believe in man's incorrigible, sinful desires. God is a despot who waits, rod in hand, for Judgment Day, when he will pardon but a few chosen ones. Calvin and John Knox are responsible for this gloomy spirit. No man can go on living with the certainty of his sinfulness and his subsequent damnation. The Highlanders in Scotland eventually withstood it and chose instead joy and unconcern as the order of the day. On Cape Breton it was not so easy to preserve this freedom and serenity of soul. Alone, cut off from the world, they succumbed to the old devil of a guilt-ridden conscience.

Their only escape from this evil is in knowledge that casts out superstition, or on the mainland where the rich opportunities for economic growth would give another direction to their thoughts and deeds.

Each Man's Son, like *Barometer Rising* is reminiscent of familiar tales from mythology. Archie MacNeil leaves the underground mines of his homeland to seek his fortune as a professional boxer in the United States. He hopes to return to his wife Mollie and their son Alan as a rich man, but is disillusioned and returns without the crown of victory. When he surprises his wife with her lover he kills them both.

It is an oft-told tale. Why should it not ring true on Cape Breton? MacLennan had the good sense to leave the Presbyterian demons out of this episode. Whether it was necessary to fall back on them to account for the character of Dr. Ainslie, another important figure in the novel, is questionable. Daniel Ainslie, in spite of his refuge in science and his pursuit of Homer in his leisure hours, was never able to escape the devil of a bad conscience. He is bothered by the fact that he likes to be with Mollie MacNeil. When he takes an interest in her son Alan, he does not trust his own motives and reproaches himself for it. To make this psychology of the Highlanders credible, MacLennan introduces a man who knows the gloomy tortured souls of his countrymen, Dr. MacKenzie, a fatherly friend of Ainslie. He has freed himself from Calvinism to a degree that borders on blasphemy, and flatly denies the Calvinists any right to call themselves Christians. True Christians rejoice in life and do not continually brood over their sinfulness. MacKenzie would like to convert his friend Ainslie to this joy in life and draw out the thorn of Puritanism: "... You feel guilty merely because you are alive, but that's what you were taught to believe until you grew up."[11] MacKenzie explains the marital discord in his friend's home as the underlying hatred that Ainslie feels towards his wife. Why hate? Because his wife was never able to wash away her husband's feeling of sinfulness. It sounds somewhat far-fetched, nor does it become more convincing when Ainslie agrees, and confesses that he has always been ashamed of the sexual desires that moved him to marry. Neither does it help to tell himself that sensuous pleasure is something beautiful and healthy. It takes him time to regain his balance, but he accepts the orphaned boy into his childless home and now that Alan's mother is dead, he can carry out this act of mercy towards a poor child with no pangs of conscience. He no longer needs to distrust himself and so is open to the possibilities of truly altruistic love.

V

Defining national characteristics and sketching ideal types of people is a pastime passionately indulged in by essayists and historians in Canada. It has been mockingly called the national weakness for artificial problems created in the retort of easy thinking. Only rarely is a novel the place for such games. They too easily lead to a tempest in a teapot. Witty remarks can blind us to reality instead of giving it form and substance. Entrusting a literary figure with the task of being a model for the national picture book is to reverse the order of things. The path to the model Canadian, who endorses the national mission of his people and shows the whole world that he is neither an Englishman nor an American, does not follow the rigid lines of a theory. If there is a path at all, then its first direction must be towards the life of the people and include the unmistakable stamp of time and place and perhaps even nationality. MacLennan has flirted long enough with national-cultural chimeras to the detriment of his novels. They remind one of a chessboard, where the typologically carved figures are moved about according to the strict rules of the game. The writer justifies himself by insisting that Canada must first get to know itself and furthermore that this self-knowledge will be found in literature quite independently of whether it be didactic or not, or even appear behind the times in comparison with the literature of other nations. They reached maturity by the same route.

But when has serious literature ever aimed exclusively at focusing on a national prototype? Creative writing that successfully portrays a people becomes itself a mirror of the very people whose language it uses. MacLennan must have realized this for he gradually turned from the frustration of trying to create powerful figures that would incorporate both the ideal and the everyday Canadian and turned to more productive themes.

We have mentioned that MacLennan is familiar with the miseries of the Depression years. He belonged to that hard-hit younger generation himself. In 1932 he left his homeland to look for work in the United States, not returning till 1938. The book about young men of 1933 that Paul Tallard wrote in *Two Solitudes* and finally threw in the fire, would give MacLennan no rest. Traces of that work are scattered throughout his novels. Paul himself is portrayed as a child of those difficult years. His struggle for mere existence rings far truer than the struggles of so many of MacLennan's characters for a Canadian national identity. In general when his characters are struggling to find work, when they are tormented by spiritual and political indecision, or when they voice strong protest against a do-nothing government and an upper class that brands all criticism as treason, then they attain a rare strength and realism. Face to face with such challenges, they ask life's ultimate questions: the meaning of existence and man's place in creation. Then their spiritual struggles ring as true as their struggle for food and shelter. MacLennan is forever setting sail with this fresh breeze at his back. The hope he stirs in us is closely allied with the hope for a work that will avoid the stagnant waters of national-cultural speculation and travel instead the proverbial "broadstream of Canadian life."

VI

MacLennan's latest novel, *The Watch that Ends the Night*, is almost completely free of the spectre of nationalism, leaving that much more room for young people around the year 1939. Although the plot is once again as old as the hills; the triangle of two men and a woman, it adapts easily to the treatment of many contemporary problems.

Catherine Chamberlain loses her first husband, Jerome Martell, in the whirlpool of those stormy years before the Second World War. Jerome bids farewell to bourgeois security and respect and places his great skill as a surgeon at the service of the Spanish Loyalists. He later disappears into the French Underground and the rumour that he was put to death by the German S.S. is eventually confirmed. Thereupon Catherine marries her former school friend, George Stewart. Her new happiness is shaken when Jerome unexpectedly turns up, but balance is restored at the end. The maturity of the two men makes such a dénouement possible, for both were completely re-cast in the crucible of the years before and after 1939. In that school of hard knocks each gained a very personal insight from his particular set of experiences. George had taught in a private school near Montreal during those lean years. Mac-Lennan's description of this ersatz English "public school" shows what a broad spectrum he has at his command. As far as his conscience will allow, George supports the fraudulent pedagogue Dr. Bigbee, who seems out of a Dickens novel. But the ironic light he puts himself in does not prevent him from overlooking the seriousness of the times. In Europe one devastating national misfortune follows upon another.

> Dolfuss [sic!] turned his artillery on the socialist apartments in Vienna while his henchmen in Styria hanged Wallisch a foot from the ground. Mussolini invaded Ethiopia and Hoare and Laval connived at it. . . . Murder exploded out of the soil of Spain and the British and the French washed their hands of it. And unemployment became no less.[12]

Meanwhile in Canada, life goes on; the sun shines, it rains, the maple leaves turn green and the sap flows. But the feeling of universal guilt for the miseries and injustices in the world never leaves George's consciousness. He is filled with a deep hatred against whole groups, but especially against those who hold the reins of government. His thoughts and feelings become more and more radical, but his development does not lead to public action. It takes place instead inside his heart and mind. This quiet self-development is rendered that much easier by the fact that he is classified as unfit for military service and so spends the war as a news commentator. MacLennan spares him so he can comment on the meaning of events, in so far as they have any meaning. George becomes quite renowned as a radio-commentator; even ministers of the government turn to him for advice. Unfortunately the reader rarely shares in these valuable insights. We hear that George has an insurmountable mistrust of all politicians who pester him with their ideologies and sovereign remedies. He is convinced that real history is being made today by the scientists, whereas politicians are only interested in their petty posts and the meaningless problems that come with them. He undertakes a trip to Russia and returns, just as Neil Macrae, Paul Tallard and Bruce Fraser did, with the conviction—it's a pity to see MacLennan back on the national culture theme—that the future, both his own, and the world's lies in Canada. Making that future a reality is to be his life's work. Besides his work at the radio station, George also teaches at McGill University in Montreal, but we are given no inkling of the content of his broadcasts or his lectures. To live counter to history, to place scientists above politicians and all the while working as a civil servant is quite an undertaking, even in liberal Canada. Fortunately MacLennan pursues his national-cultural hobby but a short time and returns to the main theme of human relationships and the road that fate has marked out for his three main characters. George may be a poor excuse for the Canadian of the future, but he is quite convincing as the defender of hearth and home, and Jerome's friend.

Jerome emerges from the crucible of the Thirties different from George. The first ten years of his life he spent in a lumber camp in New Brunswick, where he was the only child, and his mother the only woman among a group of uncivilized men. The boy often heard men's voices in his mother's room at night and her wild, abusive language as she threw out unsatisfactory lovers. One, whom she humiliated beyond all measure, retaliated by murdering her. Jerome has to flee and paddles a canoe downstream until he reaches a fair-sized town. He meets an elderly couple at the station, a country pastor and his wife, who take him with them and eventually adopt him. The shift from greed and murder (Hemingway could not have portrayed it more bluntly) to the gentle humour and piety of the pleasant atmosphere of the parsonage is one of MacLennan's greatest achievements. The pastor is reminiscent of McCunn in *The Precipice.* He shares McCunn's fondness for the bottle and his criticism of Church claims, though in milder form.

In the company of these true Christians, Jerome feels called to become the champion of God and the Gospels. It was later said that he did not renounce his religion, he only lost it. The man who loses something, hopes for recovery or replacement of the lost article. George fights fascism with an almost religious passion. The former champion of God takes up cudgels against organized brutality. Whereas his friend George, under the pressure of the world's needs, turns to independent thinking, Jerome turns to deeds. Considering it a duty in these inhuman times, he leaves wife and family to fight the dragon. No matter how lucid this decision, or how noble the reasons behind it, MacLennan is confident he sees it all from a higher vantage point. What he sees is the irrational element that clings even to men like Jerome. In the choppy currents and counter-currents of the popular front, unemployment and the Spanish Civil War, even a Jerome cannot know what is really needed and whether he is on the right road. Such international crises are in MacLennan's words gigantic mystery plays, with the politicians acting out their dark and absurd passions. The script respects neither reason nor facts. The best thing for the audience is to turn its back on it all. Is this not what Jerome does, when he tends the wounded from both sides instead of actually fighting? And even if this urge to help is the best antidote to chaos, does he weigh the cost to Jerome? Why would a good man leave his family? MacLennan manages to prejudice us against this honest world-reformer and place a question mark after the value of his deeds: Would he not have been better off to stay home with his wife and child and look after his patients?

Jerome returns home and now we shall see whether he can really give his best in his homeland. He spares us patriotic visions, probably because he mistrusts the sweep of grandiose plans. But the position he so carelessly left has been filled. His former wife and their daughter no longer need him. He is as superfluous in this small circle as he was in the larger circle of world chaos where he found he could be of no lasting use. The author had to make up very tenuous incidents to convince the reader that Jerome was needed more urgently at home than in the world's trouble spots. A minor pretext allows him entry to the house he left years before. He has the opportunity to make good his earlier neglect, and is able to do more for a few, for one human being, than he was able to do for mankind. The author brought Jerome home so he could make not life, but death, easier for his former wife.

Catherine suffered from her youth with a rheumatic heart and had repeated warnings that her life could be cut short. The excitement of her first husband returning was hardly calculated to improve her health. The fairly certain diagnosis of imminent death brings the two men together. They both avidly wish to lighten her last days and not make her death difficult. Jerome assumes the leading role.

The attack on the spectre of death comes from more than one direction. Catherine is to learn that life is something unbelievably glorious, so that even the short time left to her fills her with overwhelming joy and banishes all fear. To this end MacLennan displays the fireworks of the mysticism of light and life. Light makes us human because it triumphs over the darkness within us; light is spirit, the spirit of God that encompasses man. He who dares to walk in the light will discover what a gift life is. To have made life possible, is God's greatest glory, and with it He justifies His often fearful and unjust sovereignty over us.

> He gave life ... Life for a year, a month, a day or an hour
> is still a gift. The warmth of the sun or the caress of the air,
> the sight of a flower or a cloud on the wind, the possibility
> even for one day more to see things grow—the human bon-
> dage is also the human liberty.[13]

After that it is art that serves to give Catherine's life, short as it may be, the appearance of completion. In recent years she had reactivated her considerable talent for painting. Painting, almost as easily as music, has the power to transport us above the constraints of existence, to a state of cheerful indifference to our cares. With each picture that Catherine begins, her rapture is renewed and strengthened. With each one she completes she leaves to the world a portion of her bliss, and a happiness in which the exigencies of time dissolve and vanish.

As though this were not enough Jerome prescribes another remedy against the fear of death. His crusade against fascism eventually brought him to China. There in his prison cell, he had a vision of Christ; not the Christ of the churches and absolution but simply Christ who died and rose again. Jerome is convinced that man can do the same; die and rise again. One must live as though death were already past; free of worry and free of all fear. Catherine has always done that and now Jerome initiates George into this mystery, so that he can be her companion in this earthly life that looks to the life beyond, and help her "live her own death."

VII

These final chapters are among the best that MacLennan has written. Though they incorporate borrowings from Rilke and other sources, the impression remains that we are dealing here with deep and genuine human relationships. The three main characters unravel a knot that a mysterious reality has drawn around them. No one steps out of character to proclaim a lyrical monologue on the essence of the Canadian or similar nonsense—non-poetic motifs, as George Woodcock calls them.[14] The reader forgets that these last pages are supposed to be a defence of the thesis of "the inner chamber," where we can be of more use than out in the world. It is neither proven nor disproven and no one asks why. More serious matters intervene.

Softly and thoughtfully Catherine, George and Jerome walk together in the shadow of death. A chilling awe erases everything they once knew as idle talk, sham, obstinacy and vanity. Truth and responsibility are both the player's lines and his gestures.

One can only wish that this performance, that rings so true, might be continued in MacLennan's future writings, provided they treat not only the end of life but also the beginning and the middle. There is so much in the Canadian way of life that begs to be described. Everyday life with its human and inhuman traits has been portrayed up to now only in small vignettes. The voice of the people is seldom heard. "The great Canadian novel" has become a slogan and almost a joke, but it means nevertheless that the great Canadian novel is passionately longed for. Hope is strong because Canadians know what they need and lack; a realistic novel, which will acquaint the widely scattered people with one another; the miner with the wheat farmer, the fisherman on the Atlantic Ocean with the fisherman on the Pacific. City, country and arctic communities are still strangers to one another. Eskimos in the white ice-fields,

Indians in the woods and plains farther south, Chinese and Japanese, who occupy whole city blocks—rarely does this rich variety of people inspire writers, unless they be writers of statistics.

The Watch that Ends the Night plumbs the depths of the inner life. It also sheds much light on the external world and its wide range of activities. MacLennan knows the country and its people and should not be afraid of a broad and unaffected realism, where it is appropriate. At the same time he insists on an appreciation of man and his way of life. Even if his future works are to concentrate more on the problems of the external world instead of the inner world, he will not cease to sift problems and educate the reader. By what standard? Certainly not according to the degree of patriotic and cultural nationalistic enthusiasm. His last novel and even more his essay, "Help Thou Mine Unbelief,"[15] allay those fears. It contains his views on today's lack of faith, with no show of impatience or suggestion of conversion. If we are less mystical in our religion, we are nevertheless good-hearted in practical matters and more ready to lend a hand in the true Christian sense than people before us.

> If we on this continent have largely lost the capacity to be near to God, we have perhaps gained the capacity to be near to Jesus.[16]

When love of neighbour is missing—this is the meaning of these lines—education will have to see that everything is in order. The realistic novel is a ready instrument of true humanism. One meets at all levels people who are upright, generous and happy; such living models are the salt of reality, creating their image is the task of literature.

NOTES

1. "Literature. Part I. Poetry and the Novel," in *The Culture of Contemporary Canada*, ed. Julian Park, (Ithaca, N.Y.: Cornell University Press, 1957), p. 29.

2. *New Canadian Library*, No. 8, (Toronto, 1958). See also: Hugo McPherson, "The Novels of Hugh MacLennan," in *Queen's Quarterly*, vol. LX (1953), pp. 186-98.

3. *New Canadian Library*, No. 8, p. 79.

4. *Le Canada, Puissance Internationale* (Paris, 1937), p. 16.

5. *Two Solitudes*, (New York, 1945), p. 115.

6. "The Ghost that Haunts Us," in *Thirty and Three*, (Toronto, 1954).

7. "The Canadian Character," in *Cross-Country* (Toronto, 1949).

8. *The Precipice* (Toronto, 1948), p. 8.

9. "The Canadian Character" and "An Eagle Mewing," in *Thirty and Three.*

10. "What Makes a City," in *Thirty and Three.*

11. *Each Man's Son* (Toronto, 1951), p. 63.

12. *The Watch that Ends the Night* (New York, 1959), p. 123.

13. *The Watch that Ends the Night*, p. 344.

14. "Hugh MacLennan," in *Northern Review*, vol. III (1950), No. 4, pp. 2-10.

15. In *Cross-Country.*

16. *Cross-Country*, p. 146.

THE NOVELS OF HUGH MACLENNAN

ROBERT D. CHAMBERS

In many ways I count myself lucky to have lived in Canada
when I did. In the next generation it will become clear
that the ground here was very good for a writer in the last
eighteen years. Suddenly the thought occurs to me that the
only countries where really major themes have been tackled
during this time have been Canada and South Africa. Only
the occasional Canadian book has received a large overseas
public, but quite a few of them last. They seem to adhere. *

When Hugh MacLennan put these words into a letter in 1958, he
had just finished writing *The Watch that Ends the Night.* He was
looking back across twenty years of work, content that his time
and his place had yielded rich and enduring materials for the Canadian writer. The sequence of his novels—*Barometer Rising* (1941),
Two Solitudes (1945), *The Precipice* (1948), *Each Man's Son* (1951)
and *The Watch that Ends the Night* (1959)—testifies to the fertile
range of opportunities that a Canadian novelist could grasp in this
century.

I

Opportunities accompanied, however, by difficulties. As MacLennan
himself has pointed out, the Canada of literature has been a largely
unmapped and uncharted land. Older place names—New York, London, Rome—provide writers with a set of useful literary ciphers;
no such immediate connotations attach to Halifax, Montreal, or
Toronto. Trafalgar Square, St. Peter's and Fifth Avenue live in a
thousand books, but what of Barrington Street, St. Joseph's, and
Bay? MacLennan's first hurdle was the problem of background:

"The Novels of Hugh MacLennan," by Robert D. Chambers. In *Journal of
Canadian Studies*, 2 (August, 1967), pp. 3-11. By permission of the author
and the publisher.
*Quoted by permission of Hugh MacLennan.

> When I first thought of writing this novel [*Barometer Rising*]
> Canada was virtually an uncharacterized country. It seemed
> to me then that if our literature was to be anything but
> purely regional, it must be directed to at least two audiences.
> One was the Canadian public, which took the Canadian scene
> for granted but had never defined its particular essence. The
> other was the international public, which had never thought
> about Canada at all, and knew nothing whatever about us.[1]

The outsider must be told much that he did not know before; the
insider reacquainted with what he has long known, but made to see
it in a new way. When Paul Tallard, the young hero of *Two Solitudes*,
contemplates his first book the problems of language and background
demand early solution:

> But because it used the English and French languages, a
> Canadian book would have to take its place in the English
> and French traditions. Both traditions were so mature they
> had become almost decadent, while Canada herself was still
> raw. Besides, there was the question of background. As Paul
> considered the matter, he realized that his readers' ignor-
> ance of the essential Canadian clashes and values presented
> him with a unique problem. The background would have
> to be created from scratch if his story was to become in-
> telligible. He could afford to take nothing for granted. He
> would have to build the stage and props for his play, and
> then write the play itself.[2]

This willingness to start from scratch, to assume nothing and provide all, is the initial fact to grasp about MacLennan's fiction. It
explains why students of Canadian history and society turn to his
books for a "sense of period." The flexibility of the novel form
provided MacLennan with the chance to be "something of a geog-
rapher, an historian and sociologist,"[3] and he welcomed the opportunity. No other Canadian novels capture such a wealth of social
documentation, with the result that they have been variously interpreted, as allegories of emergent Canadian nationality (George Woodcock), or Canadian variations on a basic theme of Puritan Calvinism
(Roy Daniells), or successive stages in a revelation of Canadian consciousness (Hugo McPherson).[4]

MacLennan's novels thus look back to the more ample canvases of Thackeray and Tolstoy. In his books, character is shaped not primarily by inner-directed impulses, but by the play and interplay of those historic forces which sweep across Canadian life. If occasionally his people become puppet-like stereotypes, they are often memorable representatives of that elusive abstraction called "the Canadian character." As Arthur Lower once shrewdly remarked, "Novelists can perhaps not be too sharply blamed if they are distracted from character in the midst of so much sociology."[5]

II

What are these forces? How does MacLennan convey their pervasive effect on the character of Canadian life? It may be well, at the outset, to discover MacLennan's view of the historical process:

> It is our axiom that history is a *mélange* of determinism and accident, but a *mélange* more or less logical. . . . The *time* at which an event takes place most certainly hinges on human decision; the *manner* in which the event takes place more or less hinges on human decision. But, notwithstanding, there are tides in the affairs of men that no individual can possibly stem. There are times when the process of events is seen, with pitiless clarity, to be issuing from formal causes far remote, when individuals are like flies on a torrent, when almost everyone seems to want something not to happen, and yet later ages, looking back, see that it had to happen.[6]

Clearly MacLennan's view of history is powerfully dramatic. Men may shape events, but as often the flow of the times determines their course. It is essentially a Tolstoyan view, which sees both man and the state inheriting from the past powerful influences which press upon the present and thereby create dramatic conflict and revolutionary change. It is a view heavily overlaid with a sense of inevitability.

In Canada these forces from the past have been various—the rigid and outmoded attitudes of colonialism; the late arrival on the Canadian scene of technological and industrial advances, creating the dehumanizing rush of competitive capitalist life; the tense religious ethic of our Puritan forefathers, producing from beyond the grave a deep sense of guilt-ridden worthlessness; the mere inheritance of conventions and traditions—linguistic, racial, religious—which cramp and constrict the modern Canadian's search for himself.

To convey this dramatic conflict, MacLennan uses a device that is perennially new. Homer used it on the plains of Troy, and it was still new when Ibsen and Shaw employed it in their theatres of ideas. It might be called "generations in conflict." The old way is characterized by prejudice, selfishness, narrowness—above all, by success. Its aim is to perpetuate the vested interests of its own limited values and views. The new way stands for intelligence, tolerance, and humanity. It must resist the coercion of the old and retain its dignity somehow in the process.

This approach may seem naive or melodramatic, but it has served many writers well; moreover, it reflects MacLennan's personal conviction that the course of Canadian history and society reveals what amounts to a continuous spiritual advance:

> Young men on this continent today are gentler and kindlier
> than they were when I was young, and when I was a boy
> we were gentler and kinder than boys were in my father's
> generation. . . . People have become more considerate in their
> dealings with one another. They are more tolerant. They
> have come to feel a profound sense of responsibility toward
> the underprivileged.[7]

Whatever one thinks of this thesis, it is clear that it gives a basic unity to MacLennan's fiction: the old and the new—whether expressed as characters or social forces—are here dramatically joined.

III

MacLennan's first novel—*Barometer Rising* (1941)—has been brilliantly analyzed by Hugo McPherson.[8] I have little to add, except to note that the conflict here is between the old colonial Canada and the new independent nation just arising. MacLennan's characters are deployed to develop this theme: Geoffrey Wain representing the old order, Penny Wain and Neil Macrae the new. Several minor characters—notably Angus Murray and Alec MacKenzie—are caught between generations, and belong to neither world. In *Barometer Rising*, MacLennan solves the conflict of generations through that titanic blast of Thursday, 6 December 1917, which left Halifax "a town hideous with destruction in which more than a quarter of the population were mourners."[9] The explosion sequence, surely one of the most powerful pieces of prose ever written in Canada, takes the place of a direct confrontation between Geoffrey Wain, Alec MacKenzie, and Neil Macrae. External forces—the explosion of war and munitions ships—determine the play of characters, and the novel is allowed to conclude on a note of romantic and nationalistic hope.

In a sense, *Barometer Rising* was a rehearsal for *Two Solitudes* (1945).[10] But this second novel is considerably more ambitious: nowhere in our literature has a larger theme been attempted; nowhere a wider horizon swept. Covering twenty-two years, involving three generations, *Two Solitudes* is a profound commentary on Canadian life in the first half of the twentieth century.

The divisions of the book are important. The first two span the years 1917 to 1921: they achieve tragedy. The last two comprise the years 1934 and 1939: they see a similar tragedy averted. In the first half of *Two Solitudes*, MacLennan poses a dilemma in his analysis of Canadian life in the first quarter of this century: Canadian society was forced to make a potentially tragic choice between the old and the new. Athanase Tallard embodies that dilemma.

Emotionally attached to the agrarian life of rural Quebec, yet intelligent enough to see that Quebec's future lies with industrial development; headstrong in his anticlericalism because the clergy oppose that future, yet Catholic at heart; intent upon developing Quebec with French, not English, capital, yet ignorant of big business— Tallard is driven to the knowledge that his life can be successful only if he chooses between the old and the new. These opposed, indeed hostile, forces are depicted by the powerful interests of the Catholic and Protestant ethics. The Church, characterized by Father Beaubien, demands its traditional right to inform the intellect and guide the soul of Athanase Tallard. But Tallard rejects his tradition, moves to Montreal, turns Presbyterian, and identifies himself with the Protestant ethic, characterized by Huntly McQueen. Tallard becomes tragic when, choosing to reject the old and hoping to give meaning to his life by embracing the new, he isolates himself and dies a bankrupt and a failure. This is French Canada—possibly all Canada—attempting to rid herself of tradition by turning to worship the new God of Success, and unwittingly isolating herself because she can neither live with the new nor return to the old.

MacLennan conveys this theme in some wonderfully tense scenes between Father Beaubien and Tallard, between Tallard and Huntly McQueen. The climax is reached superbly when Tallard, rejected by McQueen and faced with total failure, finds himself alone in the empty canyon of St. James Street on the day when all Montreal has flocked north to Sherbrooke Street to cheer the soldiers returning from the war.

As Roy Daniells has remarked of *Two Solitudes*, "MacLennan has set up the board for the chess-game of Canadian society."[11] By the time of Tallard's death in 1921, one half of the game has been played: by then, the proud dreams of Father Beaubien and Athanase Tallard—bitter rivals for power in rural Quebec—have been dashed by the urban manoeuvres of a French Catholic Political Bishop and an English Protestant Industrial Knight.

In the second half of *Two Solitudes*, MacLennan poses the dilemma of the earlier sections in new terms. The new of the first half—the Protestant ethic—becomes the old of the second half. If Athanase Tallard was forced to choose between priest and businessman, his son Paul has only the businessman to confront. Paul is already emancipated from the Catholic ethic, but he does battle with its Protestant counterpart, characterized on the economic level by Huntly McQueen and on the social level by Janet Methuen.

Huntly McQueen is one of MacLennan's most memorable creations. Born in a small Ontario town in the mid-1870s, the son of a Presbyterian minister who died when Huntly was still a child, raised in Toronto on poverty and prayers, pressed on in his studies by the tenacious will of a mother whom he came to venerate, Huntly McQueen embodies the Puritan conviction that failure in the world of affairs is sinful and that success somehow glorifies a highly selective Calvinist God. After graduation from the University of Toronto, and through the opportunity created by the death of an uncle-in-business (whose passing Huntly and his mother came to regard as a divine accident which saved Huntly from becoming a professor), McQueen began to exercise his enormous skill to impose his own pattern, "his own studied technique of doing everything as unobtrusively as possible," which "trained people to expect from him nothing dramatic, nothing that stimulates the imagination, nothing that suggests a crisis."[12] Finding it a profitable thing to help Max Aitken cement the British Empire, by 1917 Huntly McQueen had become a multi-millionaire and one of the stately domes of Canada.

In the second half of *Two Solitudes*, Paul Tallard rejects the coercion of McQueen and Janet Methuen, and allies himself with Heather Methuen, a girl of sturdy independence who has emancipated herself from seeking the sort of Canadian success represented by St. James Street and Westmount. Unlike Athanase Tallard, whose life could be successful only by identification with one of two constricting powers, and unlike Marius Tallard, whose fierce devotion to the Catholic ethic led him to beat the useless drum of racial hatred, Paul and Heather take on humanity and stature by refusing to become the stereotypes indicated by their backgrounds. It is not accidental that they must first leave Canada in order to see it objectively. Returning, they know that the price of success in Canada is the loss of their individuality. Refusing to become pawns in an old and futile chess game, they represent MacLennan's belief that "the *élite* among today's youth would sooner be happy than famous, and would prefer to be loved than to be admired."[13]

The second half of *Two Solitudes* has been criticized as over-written and unconvincing, and it is interesting to note that MacLennan has allowed some pruning for the paperback and school editions. Nevertheless, the later parts of the novel carry through his vigorous assault on the pillars of Canadian respectability, and his closing picture of intelligent Canadian youth facing with tolerance and humanity the problems of their generation seems made of stuff that will adhere.

IV

In MacLennan's two following novels—*The Precipice* (1948) and *Each Man's Son* (1951)—the conflict of old and new is continued, but with a difference. Both books convey the agonizing limitations imposed on human personality by the Calvinist creed. MacLennan's problem here—one shared by Sinclair Ross and Ernest Buckler in their treatments of this theme—is that of representation: the characters, we are constantly told, are closely pursued by the hound of heaven, but we never see the beast. With the exception of Jane Cameron in *The Precipice*, who is the Calvinist creed made flesh, MacLennan's characters in these two books suffer from a nameless anguish: austere and lonely, they struggle to understand that the will of God cannot be done while they are frightened and ashamed of themselves.

Their most memorable representative is Daniel Ainslie in *Each Man's Son*. A dedicated surgeon in the coal-mining town of Broughton, near Sydney in Cape Breton, Ainslie is held fast by the grip of an ancient curse, branded on his soul by a harsh and unforgiving father, and little mitigated by a submissive and self-sacrificing mother. Fiercely wedded to medicine in a community of almost total misery, Ainslie is bitterly aware that his great talent is wasted. He disguises his sense of disgraced worthlessness by stern service to his work. His only escape is typically Puritan. He takes the first of two conventional outlets—learning and liquor. (Broughton's miners take the liquor.) Yet Ainslie's study of Homeric Greek is a task enforced. His blinkered vision dramatically illustrates Tawney's famous analogy: "The Puritan is like a steel spring compressed by an inner force, which shatters every obstacle by its rebound. Sometimes the strain is too tense, and, when its imprisoned energy is released, it shatters itself."

In the character of Daniel Ainslie, and in his salvation through the understanding love of a mature woman, MacLennan pursues the struggle of a highly self-conscious Puritan to free himself from fear of Calvin's wrathful God. That the struggle toward self-knowledge must be painful, that a reconciliation with life can be won, is the lesson that Ainslie finds harder to master than Homer or neuro-surgery:

> They were criminals, the men who had invented the curse
> and inflicted it upon him, but they were all dead. There
> was no one to strike down in payment for generations of
> cramped and ruined lives. The criminals slept well, and
> their names were sanctified.[14]

MacLennan's implication is clear: Puritans must suffer if they allow
dead men to make them ashamed of themselves.

V

Shortly before the publication of *The Watch that Ends the Night*
(1959), MacLennan gave notice that his new novel was a departure
from previous practice:

> This book is just as international as a book written with the
> scene laid in London or Paris or New York or Rome. The
> characters in the book are (all of them except a few English-
> men who are minor characters and appear briefly) all Cana-
> dian. And I think the Montreal background is very important.
> I have a great affection for Montreal and, in a way, it be-
> comes one of the principal characters in the book. But there
> wasn't any attempt to analyze Canada here. I used to do
> that when it seemed necessary to make a map before you
> could put a story in it.[15]

MacLennan would argue that, with the maturing of Canadian fiction
since the war years, his approach to novel writing has been allowed
to change. He now regards the specifically Canadian content as a
happy by-product, not as a point of departure. He has expanded his
views on this point in an essay called "Literature in a New Country."
Here he entertains the analogy that about 1940 Canadian literature
passed beyond colonial status, as American literature had done a
century earlier with Melville and Hawthorne. Canada's continued
regionalism up to that time is indicated by our writers' attention to
landscape, not to people and cities. MacLennan argues that Cana-

dian writers had to wait for their society to shed its colonial characteristics:

> No writer can jump the gap until his society has grown
> across it like a bridge; until the spirit of his society has
> merged with that of the world. The impatient young writer
> in a new country does well to remember that time is the
> essence of his and his country's problem, just as he should
> also remember that although on occasion his province may
> be a hindrance to him, it is literally all that he has behind
> him. Shakespeare's England was once a province, too; so was
> Tolstoy's Russia. One of literature's chief tasks is to bridge
> the gap between province and heartland, to merge the spiri-
> tual and moral life of the province with that of the core.
> But he cannot do this singlehanded. He cannot do this until
> the time is ripe and the province, outgrowing its old spiri-
> tual dependence, becomes old enough to consent to be its
> own judge.[16]

As province and heartland merge, there arises a new literary maturity. Moreover, MacLennan would draw a parallel in time between his own development as a novelist and the leap which Canadian literature has achieved in the postwar years from colonial to international status. The earlier need to write the play and then build the stage props has radically changed: the literary land is more fully mapped, and the writer can assume more extensive familiarity on the reader's part. This new sense of freedom lies behind MacLennan's suggestion that a theoretical difference separates *The Watch that Ends the Night* from his earlier novels.[17] MacLennan's grasping of this new opportunity can be seen in the following passage, in which George Stewart recalls the summer of his first love for Catherine:

> So that summer I entered Arcadia and the pipes played
> and the glory of the Lord shone round about. The colors of
> that summer's end are with me yet: the heavy greens of the
> land and the lighter greens of the gardens, the pinks of the
> phlox and the ripening apples, the scarlets and tulip-yellows
> of tremendous sunsets when the clouds stood high as the
> Himalayas over the pastel-colored lake where yachts lay

becalmed. Even the nights were visible. They were dark velvet before the moon rose and later, when the moon was up, Catherine and I along the shore smelled the sedge and the plants, the summer smells of growth and decay, and I thought of her as a whiteness in the dusk.

But that summer more happened to us than falling in love. If childhood is a garden, the gates closed on us then and ever afterwards we were on the outside, on the outside even of the community in which we were born.

Montreal is a world-city now with most of the symptoms of one, but in those days it was as a visiting Frenchman described it, an English garrison encysted in an overgrown French village. We belonged to the outer fringes of this garrison where the soldiering was done in the banks and trust houses and national insurance companies, the generals being the board chairmen, while the lower officers were the executives who kept things running. The English-speaking garrison of Montreal, absolutely sure of itself in the heart of the French island in North America, was a place where people knew most of the things they needed to know without having to think at all. If you were born in it, and your nature fitted it, your path was clear from childhood. Catherine and I were born in it, but neither of us fitted, and neither did our families.[18]

The movement of this passage is subtle and fascinating. It begins with the universal fact of falling in love: there is no specific background; Catherine and George are every young woman and man. The second paragraph, alluding quietly to Adam and Eve's expulsion from the Garden, shifts attention from the world of natural growth and innocence to the world of social fact. In the third paragraph, it would not seem to matter if the reader doesn't know the specific historical background of the English garrison in the heart of a French village. He will read it as a typical piece of anti-Establishment writing. By providing a vaguely associative frame of reference, MacLennan enables Catherine and George to become broadly symbolic of all those—Canadian or otherwise—who don't "belong."[19]

Unlike the people of his earlier books, here the characters do not seem mechanically deployed to illustrate specific forces at work in Canadian life. The Depression was of course not merely a Canadian phenomenon, and although George Stewart and Jerome Martell may represent contrasting aspects of Canadian character, their primary senses of identity transcend national patterns. Not that *The Watch that Ends the Night* isn't firmly rooted in Canadian experience, for MacLennan evokes memorably Laurentian lakes, the forests and rivers of New Brunswick, and especially the city of Montreal—really two Montreals, the one of the 1930s from its entrenched medical elite through left-wing academic circles to bloody political rallies, explosions of protest amidst hunger, disease, and despair; and the other postwar Montreal, financially secure and complacent, competently bureaucratic, quietly living unto itself under the lengthening shadow of the bomb.

Moreover, there are some obvious parallels with MacLennan's previous books; masculine heroism is chiefly exemplified in the fields of war and medicine, and women's courage is still expressed through creative human relationships.[20]

The surprising new element in *The Watch that Ends the Night* is its narrative technique. The book's superbly controlled pattern of past-present counterpoint recalls MacLennan's structural achievements in *Barometer Rising* and *Each Man's Son*; in addition, MacLennan creates George Stewart, his initial experiment with a first-person narrator. Stewart focuses our interest not only on the major characters—Catherine and Jerome—but equally upon himself.

An insecure and clumsy lad who badly fails his first opportunity to experience genuine love, humilated by a series of disconnected and degrading Depression jobs, Stewart finds himself unable to respond to Jerome's idealistic and almost violent espousal of the Spanish cause:

> He said slowly and heavily: "A man must belong to something larger than himself. He must surrender to it. God was so convenient for that purpose when people could believe in Him. He was so safe and so remote." A wistful smile.

"Now there is nothing but people. In Russia our generation is deliberately sacrificing itself for the future of their children. That's why the Russians are alive. That's why they're happy. They're not trying to live on dead myths."[21]

But George remains quietly sceptical of heroism, recognizing a deeper need for a home and family. Jerome's departure for Spain, and the subsequent revelation that he has been tortured to death by the Nazis in 1941, allows George to marry Catherine and achieve what Adam Blore had earlier predicted:

"You know, George, you're that very rare thing, a perfect specimen. You're middle class to the bone. You're a nice guy. All you want is a nice little wife and a nice little apartment and a nice little job, and yet you hang around with these hot-shots that hang around me. You're about as revolutionary as Stanley Baldwin."[22]

Appearances to the contrary, George is not the anti-heroic little man. A chance job with the CBC in 1939 catapults him to national prominence as a wartime news commentator.

Marriage to Catherine, and paternal care of Sally, the child of Catherine's previous marriage to Jerome, seems to have fulfilled his dream of the green isle that needs must be:

Happiness did not come to Catherine and me in a rush; rather it grew like summer weather after a cool spring in a northern land. I heard her laughing again, I watched her face shed some of its lines and grow younger again, I saw a new ease with the growing Sally. . . . She had been lost and now she was found. As I, lost for years, had also been found. As the world, apparently lost for more than a decade, now seemed to be finding itself, too.[23]

It is this quiet dream of secure love (as Catherine says, "If only the world would leave us alone, our days would be paradise") that is shattered by Jerome's sudden return as from the dead, a *revenant* which precipitates the spiritual crisis of the novel and reveals George Stewart agonistes—a Hamlet with the features of Horatio.[24]

One is not facetious in suggesting a parallel in character between George Stewart and Hamlet. For in *The Watch that Ends the Night*, MacLennan makes an approach to the traditional territory of painful self-discovery and slow, hard-won regeneration. Jerome, Catherine, and George find the wellsprings of new life in what is essentially a religious source: in a different way, each lives under the sword of Damocles; each discovers that all loving is the loving of life in the midst of death; each learns to value the mystery that other ages have so confidently called God.

The animus against Establishment hypocrisy and stupidity which led MacLennan earlier to create Geoffrey Wain, Huntly McQueen, and Janet Methuen is here replaced by a mature acceptance of the inner light that can irradiate a very un-ideal outer world. George Stewart grows beyond a mere expression of his generation, Canadian or otherwise, and Catherine, a symbol of immanence in a world beset by danger and death, subsumes the nostrums and idealisms of the earlier novels.[25]

VI

Edmund Wilson has called MacLennan the "secretary of society."[26] Looked at in one light, it may seem a description which damns with faint praise: secretaries rather earnestly keep an eye on things, dully recording the minutiae of diurnal circumstances. But without this drab process, the passing scene is erased forever from human memory. Posterity may feel cause to be grateful for Hugh MacLennan's efforts, and his leading qualities seem to me of a kind to keep his work in the forefront of our literary tradition. He has a rare capacity to see the places of Canada vividly in terms of their geographical and historical contexts, and to chart the movements of men and ideas against this natural background, so that the Halifax, Cape Breton, Quebec, and Montreal of English Canadian literature are cities and regions of his creation. Through a process of gradual maturing, not without its disappointments and failures, he has moulded characters at once recognizably indigenous and approaching—in his later work—universal significance. He has likewise sharpened our awareness of the powerful forces at work in this century, often revealing the hitherto hidden sources of our fear and loneliness as a people, bringing to light the fact of our quiet and surprising heroism. All of this he has conveyed in a direct and often didactic tone, in books of a conservative and unobtrusive technical cast, at once intellectually compelling and emotionally compassionate, and all broadly suggestive of not only our national but common and human concerns.

NOTES

1. "Where Is My Potted Palm?," *Thirty and Three* (Toronto: Macmillan, 1954), pp. 51,52. By permission of the publisher.

2. *Two Solitudes* (New York: Duell, Sloan and Pearce, 1945), p. 329. Paul's metaphor recurs in the essay mentioned in the note above: "He [the Canadian novelist] must therefore do more than write dramas, he must also design and equip the stage on which they were to be played." (p. 52)

3. See note 1: p. 52.

4. For Woodcock: *Northern Review*, No. 3 (1950), pp. 2-10, and *Canadian Literature*, no. 10 (1961), pp. 7-18 (reprinted in *Masks of Fiction*, ed. A. J. M. Smith, Toronto: McClelland and Stewart, 1961, pp. 128-40). For Daniells: article on Canadian literature in *The Culture of Contemporary Canada*, ed. Julian Park (Ithaca: Cornell U.P., 1957), pp. 1-80. For McPherson: *Queen's Quarterly*, 60 (1953), pp. 186-98; "Introduction" to *Barometer Rising*, New Canadian Library, 8 (Toronto; McClelland and Stewart, 1958); review of *The Watch that Ends the Night* in the *Daily Star* (Toronto, Feb. 21, 1959), p. 32; and "Fiction (1940-1960)" in *Literary History of Canada*, ed. Carl Klinck (Toronto: Univ. of Toronto Press, 1965), pp. 694-722.

5. In a review of *Two Solitudes* from the *Canadian Historical Review* (Sept. 1945), pp. 327-28.

6. "Roman History and To-Day," *Dalhousie Review*, 15 (1936), pp. 70-71, published the year following MacLennan's graduation with the Ph.D. in classical history from Princeton.

7. "Help Thou Mine Unbelief," *Cross-Country* (Toronto: Collins, 1949), pp. 146-47.

8. See note 4 above.

9. *Barometer Rising* (New York: Duell, Sloan and Pearce, 1941), p. 313.

10. This is suggested by the somewhat similar roles of Geoffrey Wain and Huntly McQueen, Angus Murray and Athanase Tallard, Penny Wain and Heather Methuen, Neil Macrae and Paul Tallard.

11. See note 4 above.

12. "The Canadian Character," *Cross-Country*, pp. 3-4. These quotations refer to Mackenzie King; they apply equally well to McQueen, whom MacLennan readily admits was modelled on King.

13. "Being Middle-Aged," *Thirty and Three*, p. 245.

14. *Each Man's Son* (Toronto: Macmillan, 1951), p. 219.

15. From an interview in the Toronto *Telegram* (Feb. 21, 1959), p. 33. Copyright, Toronto *Telegram*.

16. "Literature in a New Country," *Scotchman's Return* (Toronto: Macmillan, 1960), pp. 140-41. Reprinted by permission. Readers will note the interesting use of "old" and "new" in this passage. See also a letter quoted by Roy Daniells (note 4 above), p. 29.

17. See "The Story of a Novel," which began as a CBC talk, appeared in *Canadian Literature*, No. 3 (1960), and has been reprinted in *Masks of Fiction*, ed. A. J. M. Smith (Toronto, 1961), pp. 33-38.

18. *The Watch that Ends the Night* (Toronto: Macmillan, 1959), pp. 60-61.

19. The Canadian Establishment has recently been surveyed by John Porter in *The Vertical Mosaic* (Toronto, 1965). An astute fictional treatment of the Montreal Establishment, to which MacLennan is clearly indebted in *Two Solitudes*, is Gwethalyn Graham's *Earth and High Heaven* (New York, 1944).

20. For war and medicine, see Neil Macrae, Angus Murray, Daniel Ainslie, and Jerome Martell; for female heroism see Penny Wain, Lucy Cameron, Margaret Ainslie, and Catherine Stewart.

21. *The Watch that Ends the Night*, pp. 270-71.

22. *Ibid.*, p. 132.

23. *Ibid.*, p. 320.

24. Douglas LePan's brilliant description of Canadian character; quoted by Robertson Davies in *Saturday Night* (March 28, 1959), p. 29.

25. This mixture of national and universal, of province and heartland, will also inform MacLennan's forthcoming novel *Return of the Sphinx*, of which he writes: "... its basic subject is the most urgent one in the world today—the split between generations. It's as though what we have lived through in Canada in the last few years, especially in Montreal, made it possible to achieve here the sharpest focus of the world crisis."

26. *The New Yorker* (Nov. 14, 1964), p. 99.

THE STORM AND AFTER

IMAGERY AND SYMBOLISM IN HUGH MACLENNAN'S
BAROMETER RISING

WILLIAM H. NEW

Hugh MacLennan's first novel, *Barometer Rising* (1941), is important in Canadian fiction for its interpretation of the national character and for the narrative technique which it uses. Its structure is
allegorical; the two generations into which the central characters
divide, for example, represent the young Canada and the controlling
Great Britain; the explosion which figures as a prominent event in
the story represents both the First World War and the political sever-
ance between Canada and Britain, which historically accompanied
it.[1] The novel is also a work that can be read with interest outside
Canada, for the conflict that it depicts is ultimately not limited by
national boundaries.

The most vivid writing in the whole book is that which concerns
the explosion, but ironically this is in a sense an artistic flaw, for it
fixes attention on an event that, albeit spectacular, is not organically
the climax of the novel. The book is set in Halifax, Nova Scotia,
during the winter of 1917. At that time a munitions ship did blow
up in the harbour, destroying much of the town, and this was in
fact followed by a severe snowstorm which impeded rescue opera-
tions. The novel is concerned with the week of these occurrences
and with the lives of the characters as they become related, yet the
climax to which it builds is not the explosion but the invading storm.
Throughout the novel, MacLennan carefully establishes the conditions necessary for a winter storm, but this does not ultimately
result in artificial and manipulated scenes. The records of weather
assist in the evocation of mood, and the four related strands of
imagery—weather, war, diurnal change, and seasonal change (which
includes an opposition between desert and garden)—assist both in

"The Storm and After: Imagery and Symbolism in Hugh MacLennan's *Barometer Rising*," by William H. New. In *Queen's Quarterly*, 74 (Summer,
1967), pp. 302-13. Published in *Articulating West* by W.H. New (Toronto:
New Press, 1971). Reprinted by permission of the author and the publisher.

the delineation of character and in the outline of the conflict to be resolved.

The force of the explosion is such that it suggests not simply a political separation, however, but a revolutionary break. To focus on the explosion would be to emphasize revolution, yet this was neither Canada's experience nor what MacLennan suggests is a valuable course of action. It is not, that is, the pattern of development which the characters themselves in this novel, or the young nation, work out as a resolution to their conflict. The break itself is therefore still preliminary to the activity that will mean success or ruin. The explosion is disastrous but does not totally destroy the city; the snowstorm, by contrast, is ravaging, and its corollary could easily be desolation rather than freedom. What happens at that time is what allows an evolutionary development and what offers a hope for the growth of a valid national consciousness.

The young—perhaps the potential—nation is represented by four characters: Penny Wain, a ship designer whom the war had liberated from outdated and constricting attitudes, her energetic but hot-headed cousin Neil Macrae, their illegitimate daughter Jean, and Penny's brother Roddie. The old order in Canada is the older generation: Penny's father, Geoffrey, whose experiences in war have all been aimed at his personal aggrandizement, and her aunt and uncle, Alfred and Maria. The cast of central characters is completed by a third group, which includes Jim and Mary Fraser and Angus Murray. This exists on the periphery of the main action but, as a reservoir of liberal thought, it must necessarily be present if evolutionary development is to occur. When the novel begins, Neil is presumed killed in the war in Europe, but he has in fact just returned to Halifax to try to clear his name. This mission on which he had disappeared was a stupid one, and of Geoffrey's design, but Geoffrey has transferred the blame for its failure from himself to his nephew. The young man therefore faces court martial if he is discovered, and his isolation, partly self-imposed and partly imposed upon him, prevents him from at once approaching those who could really help him.

Isolation is not his affliction alone. It is also that of the other major figures and of Halifax itself, which, when Neil returns, has been set up as a garrison town. To find an internal harmony is the problem of them all. The people must come to cooperate with each other; the harbour, which "is the reason for the town's existence,"[2] must re-establish a code of marine courtesy when darkness, fog and storm disrupt it. The winter wartime setting at once connects two of the major strands of imagery. The city can defend itself against a naval attack, but when the invasion that takes place is one of weather, the defences are of no use.

* * *

A key to the function of the weather imagery is found early in the book when Angus Murray considers

> ... the way Halifax had of seeming not so much a town as
> a part of the general landscape; its chameleon-like power
> of identifying itself with the weather. There were fine days
> with westerly winds and you could smell the odour of spruce
> trees. ... But there were almost as many wet days when
> Halifax was worse than any town he could remember, when
> the fog isolated it from the ocean and the forests. ...

The isolation prevents an appropriate course of action from being either adopted or even clearly perceived, and when Neil wanders aimlessly through his town, he experiences the same problem; the "wind had changed and now it was bringing in the fog." By juxtaposing scenes, MacLennan shows a comparable situation elsewhere; Penny stands at the Shipyards, "watching the evening draw in over the water. It was invading the Stream like a visible and moving body....She stood quite still, alone in her unlighted office." As it moves in on the harbour, it moves in on her, for "this harbour with its queer congeries of the very new and the very old ... was ...a part of her life...." Angus recognizes a similar relationship in the Wain house itself: "In its silence he could hear the rhythmic pulsating of the fog signals coming in from the harbour which had given this old house its reason for life." But, with change, the order of both the house and the harbour is being challenged.

Order exists in summer and in light, therefore, but at the beginning of *Barometer Rising*, in the early winter of 1917, this light exists essentially only in memory. When Neil returns, for example, Halifax "seemed to have lost all its graciousness, and yet nothing was actually changed. Then he realized that he had been remembering it as it was in the summer with the . . . limes towering their shade over the roofs." The attunement between Penny and Neil that is made explicit later in the novel is even now worked out in the imagery. In her attitude and her occupation, Penny is alone without Neil, and her present war work seems shallow and monotonous when compared with the stability of the past:

> The anaesthetic of hard work could never compensate for the feeling of life and growth that had departed from her; and now, like a man in the desert obsessed by thoughts of green grass and running water, she remembered things as they had been before the war. . . . She recollected the odour of lime trees heavy in the streets on close summer nights when there were shooting stars, and how those evenings as she walked alone it had been possible to imagine an aeon of tranquillity broadening out like a sea under the sky, herself growing old gently, with children about her, the land where she had been born mellowing slowly into maturity.

Both Neil and Penny, then, at the beginning of the novel, are living in the past; what the conflict that forms the story does is force them away from this attitude and into another. Neil's "peculiar tenacity which made him determined to preserve himself for a future which gave no promise of being superior to the past" is paradoxically founded upon his memory of the summertime happiness, and the future is not secure until his present existence is established legally. Even then it is Angus Murray's action rather than his own that secures it. At the end of the novel, however, Penny and Neil are together, and in that moment is a consummation of all past and all future.

Before that time, there is only separation--caused by preconceived attitudes and presumed death, by darkness, by fog, and by temporal distance from summer's growth. When Penny looks out from her father's home, the darkness will not let her see clearly:

the earth was frozen hard and the flower beds were stiff
with frost. It was impossible to see the details of the garden
with its stone wall separating it from the street, its great
lime trees like buttresses beside the house-walls, its benches
and summer-house in the distant corner. The garden was the
only part of the property she really loved; to her, the rest
of the house was an incubus.

Again the relationship to summer is underlined. In the attack on
the incubus, too, is an implication that true love contains the life
and the growth which seem to have departed. In this lies the
basis for the dénouement of the novel.

The garden imagery is extended in two directions in the "Tuesday" section of the novel—one episode concerning Penny, and the
other, Neil. Prince's Lodge, the home of Jim and Mary Fraser, is a
sort of perpetual garden, one with the stones and the forest from
which it was cut, and part of the life of those who dwell there. It
is to the Frasers that Penny can turn for a home for Jean, to them
that she can look for support and sympathy in her relationships
with Neil and Angus. Prince's Lodge becomes, as it were, the rest-
ing spot in her desert, for it seems "an oasis of yellow light in the
brooding and heavy darkness of the forest." Neil, too, is further involved both with his memory of the summer garden of love and
with the present bleak winter: "The strange sense of peace grew as
he watched the sun roll over the line of trees by the Wanderers'
Grounds and disappear in fire. . . Even as he stood and watched,
the colours were dying, and by the time he had reached Spring
Garden Road again it was dark." For Neil as for Penny, darkness
threatens the vision, and the knowledge of fullness, which they had
found in love in Montreal "at the zenith of the [summer] season"
and "in the dawn together," is only a transitory peace when they
are apart.

An ironic twist is given to Penny's relationship with Jean during
this particular episode at Prince's Lodge:

Penny was bending over her, beginning the evening tale.
"When the winter comes and Jean goes out in the woods,

she can't see a thing but the white blanket of snow that
covers everything. But underneath the snow there are all
sorts of things happening. The rabbits have cities in the
ground with tunnels all made like little streets and big holes
where they live, warm like you are now, until the spring
comes and the snow melts. . . ."
"Bees and bears, Aunt Penny?"
"Oh, when the snow falls they just go sound asleep and they
never wake up at all, not till after it all melts away."

The peaceful blanket of the tale is soon to come in reality as a
blizzard, and sleeping is soon to be a grim euphemism for death—
all this unknowingly on Penny's part and therefore ironic in its
foreshadowing. Almost immediately, Angus and Penny leave in the
night, and a hint is given as to the course that disaster will take: the
"forest was hushed on the verge of winter storms." When Penny then
turns to Angus upon arrival back in Halifax and says, "Thank you for
giving me this afternoon," the ambivalence of image and heartfelt
commonplace underlines the portent of difficulties to come.

Penny, of course, is aware that what she tells Jean is superficially
unreal, but what she does not recognize is that her own dream of
the past—a never-never land of the has-been and the might-have-
been—has similar qualities of the fairytale about it. In a different
way this is the same difficulty that attends the attitudes of Geoffrey,
Alfred, and Maria Wain. They apparently live in the present—and
even for the future, as the Colonel's plan for a military oligarchy
would seem to indicate—but the basis for their thinking belongs
to the past. It emanates from nineteenth-century Britain rather
than from the land and the time in which they live.

This division is that on which MacLennan builds the emotionally
involved didactic passages in the novel. When Neil moves down
Spring Garden Road in the darkness, the point has already been
made that he has only two choices: complete success, with legal
re-establishment, or failure. For him there can be no part-way, and
this situation is also worked out in the imagery:

He wished it were spring. But the trouble was that Canada
had no proper spring; that season was always skipped when

winter leaped right into summer. One week there would
be snow-flurries and then, toward the end of May, it would
be blazing summer with the leaves unfurling on the trees. . . .

When he comes, then, to consider the future possible for himself
and his nation, he still does so without having established the present securely. Until this is done, any plans for the future, though
important, remain to some extent as idyllic and ironic as Penny's
fairytale. But the future he envisages is one that contains both darkness and light; it is one where an infinite diversity is still held together by a potent binding force. He becomes eloquent in praise
of the country he hopes to see established, but the importance of
the passage is fictional rather than political.[3] He contemplates the
"railway line, that tenuous thread which bound Canada to both
the great oceans and made her a nation, [that] lay with one end
in the darkness of Nova Scotia and the other in the flush of a British
Columbian noon." The new nation must in some way be able to
survive not only in the light, but also in the presence of acknowledged darkness. To complete the fictional pattern in *Barometer
Rising*, each of the central characters must also come through his
conflict to a new light, or else be destroyed.

* * *

There is a structural relationship between Neil's observation of sunset at the Wanderers' Grounds and Murray's visit to Mamie's brothel.
Murray's pessimism at this time, however, is in sharp contrast to
Neil's awakened enthusiasm, and it serves to illustrate an essential
difference between them:

> "What do you think of this country . . .? Everyone comes
> and goes around here, eh? So, like the wanderer, the sun
> gone down, darkness be over me, my rest a stone—that's
> your Nova Scotian, if you've the eye to see it. Wanderers.
> Looking all over the continent for a future. But they always
> come back."

Yet Angus moves away from both irony and his own isolation when
he involves himself positively in bringing Penny and Neil back
together. Neil's isolation, too, must of course also be ended before

any unity can be established. He must believe in Penny as she believes in him; he must trust Angus Murray; he must not let preconceived attitudes prevent a concerted effort to establish the truth about his military experience and thereby secure a basis upon which to build a future. Penny recognizes this, but when she invites Murray to talk to him, Neil reacts with anger and distrust. MacLennan's imagery is consistent: " 'Neil,' Penny said, 'please don't stand in your own light.' "

The loneliness of Colonel Wain is another matter. In his self-imposed, anachronistic, colonial attitude to Canada, he does not and will not admit that development is taking place. His own house reflects this refusal; from 1812 to 1917 nothing had changed; "the Wain fortune had remained stationary." Yet this occurs at a time when the traditional British dominance is giving way to a growing cosmopolitanism in the Halifax harbour—and, by extension, in the life of the town's younger generation. When Penny recognizes that the harbour "was so much a part of her life," she is watching a

> freighter sliding upstream: a commonplace ship, certainly
> foreign and probably of Mediterranean origin, manned by
> heaven knew what conglomeration of Levantines, with may-
> be a Scotsman in the engine-room and a renegade Nova
> Scotian somewhere in the forecastle. The war had brought
> so many of these mongrel vessels to Halifax, they had be-
> come a part of the landscape.

The new world is a changing one, and in the lives of Penny, Neil, Angus, and even the modified Aunt Maria, the spirit of change finds, in varying degree, an appropriate environment. Unable to admit the truth of change, however, Geoffrey wants to get away from what he considers colonial and—therefore—second-rate. Yet paradoxically he can also perceive certain values in the Nova Scotian, and despite what he says, he is disturbed when these are slighted. Nova Scotians "faced danger every day in the foggiest and stormiest tract of the entire Atlantic, and apart from the Scandinavians they were almost the only seamen still left under sail." The ability to move unscathed through darkness, fog, and storm is the very quality he himself lacks, and inwardly he had recognized but at once rejected this on the day that his ill-planned military operation failed. That he should be found dead after the explosion in the middle of the night and during a blizzard seems, though a trifle too convenient for a success-ful novel, a singularly appropriate end.

The blizzard, besides being a matter of recorded historical fact, is a focal point for the novel and is neither anticlimactic nor ex-traneous to the imagery and the action. MacLennan tabulates the weather for each day,[4] and the climax of the blizzard brings to-gether all four major strands of imagery. The Sunday of the book's opening suggests that weather from the west is more clement than that from the east. The mirage of summer which is observed there, however, is accompanied and modified by the colours of blood and disaster. Both foreshadow the course that the story will take: "Above the horizon rim the remaining light was a turmoil of rose and saffron and pallid green, the colours of blood and flowers and the sheen of sunlight on summer grass. . . . This western land was [Neil's] own country." Fog then sets in for the night. On the Monday the wind, "baffling slightly but cold and northerly," is predominantly from the cold polar high rather than from the south. It is still shifting on the Tuesday, with the marine high taking precedence and the clouds blowing to the east: "The morning was dry and crisp, the ground frozen hard, and white clouds rushed through a glittering sky out to sea." On the Wednesday, air currents begin to rise, and along the front—the war imagery being congruent here with that of the weather—conditions for the low pressure area and the storm are establishing themselves: "A pack of cumulus cloud was building up over the land across the harbour and the wind was hauling toward the south."

When the munitions ship explodes on the Thursday, the weather is still fair, but with the sun comes a strange calm that Mary Fraser thinks "almost like Indian summer." But "Jim looked at the tree-tops, motionless in the still air, and then he sniffed loudly. 'There's east in that wind.' " Under these conditions the energy of the ex-plosion is released, damaging property, killing and injuring thou-sands. Its importance here—like that of the war it represents—is that apparent logic is suspended. Back parts of houses blow down when the forces come to the front; those that escape the initial impact of wind damage are injured by debris falling from the sky; stoves which are lighted to protect people from the cold are overturned and ignite destructive fires. But the forces of the explosion are in a long view momentary, soon spent; what demands more attention is the disillusionment that can accompany a postwar period. What requires more time is the process of rehabilitation. Here, for survival of the peace, both logic and love are vital.

* * *

It is probably at the allegorical level that *Barometer Rising* would be of most interest outside Canada itself. The political ideas embodied in the work may overlap those of other developing nations, for example, but, more important here, MacLennan has demonstrated a competent use of one fictional technique for expressing them. His work insists not that a new nation be established, but that the establishment of the new nation take into account both the pangs that bring it into existence and the subsequent difficulties of salvage, repair, development, and change. The necessarily heterogeneous group that is the new nation can work in voluntary harmony only for a time; after that, the capacities of each individual must be exercised. In fictional terms, this is worked out during the blizzard when Neil considers his city:

> It occurred to him how solitary an organism Halifax had
> been. . . . Now in the End nothing remained but snow and
> an anonymous death, . . . no lights but an occasional
> lantern flickering in the darkness. There had been one splen-
> did, full-throated bellow of power: the earth had trembled,
> houses fallen, fires arisen. There had been a few hours of
> brave and passionate co-operation of human beings labouring
> in a single cause; then a mechanical routine; then exhaustion
> and hunger; then finally the primal solitude of snow . . .
> obscuring the quick and the dead . . . , of handfuls of men
> too tired to speak standing mutely in a ruined house. . . .

But if the breakdown of harmony leads to insularity, then the society ceases to be productive. Hence the last part of the novel shows the three major characters moving out of their loneliness into participation in the new order.

Each of them survives the relatively superficial injury he sustains during the explosion. Penny is the most seriously hurt, but the image that is used at this time at once indicates that she will survive: "She was on that old sofa they always set up in the garden in summer and kept in the storeroom in winter." A new order is set up in the Wain household; furniture is changed about, strangers have a freer access to those who live there. But it is only at the time of the snowstorm that Angus accepts his role as doctor again. Only then does Neil realize that he does not desire revenge; only then does he demonstrate his ability to lead. Penny, too, faces at this time the deaths of her father and the Frasers, and survives because of her love for Roddie, Neil, and Jean. This development is reflected in the storm imagery itself, for the brilliant sunlight that shone at the time of the explosion soon dulls, and the dullness rapidly develops into snow. The darkness, the desert, the weather, and the war are brought together climactically: "The wind shattered the snow high in the air and when the flakes reached the ground they had the consistency of sand. . . . The snow fell invisibly in the darkest night anyone in Halifax could remember." Invasion has come: "In the dawn the harbour was bleak and steel-coloured, extending into the whitened land like a scimitar with broken edges. . . ."

The implications of the explosion—of the political break—are not realized until it is a *fait accompli*. Only Neil's capacity to lead and Murray's ability to mend and to strengthen allow the new order then to survive. Squalls continue throughout the weekend, but certainty of future success comes late on the Saturday night, when Angus anticipates in dream a coming summer: "He saw green trees under the sun and heard locusts shrilling at high noon and there was no more snow because it was midsummer . . . " Such an expectation counteracts not only the fact of the storm, but also the reliving in memory of past summers, which had formerly been the sole way to apprehend life. On the Monday night, the weather clears.

MacLennan then goes on to underline once more the idea that has been revealed in the structural patterning of imagery throughout the novel: that in love there is a solution to the separateness of the individual. In 1941, when *Barometer Rising* was published, the author could not end the conflict completely. Penny, for example, "could see nothing clearly ahead. To force one's self on into the darkness to keep one's integrity as one moved—that was all that mattered because this was all there was left." But together, in love, in unity, Neil and Penny can maintain their new world. When, in the garden of Prince's Lodge, Neil looks beyond her "to the patch of moonlight that broke and shivered in the centre of the Basin, and heard in the branches of the forest behind him the slight tremor of a rising wind," the total darkness of the winter night is behind them, the harbour is quiet, the storm past, and the barometer can rise once more.

The images involving weather, war, and the oppositions between light and dark, summer and winter, and garden and desert are consistently and subtly patterned to support the political level at which the novel can be interpreted. Yet a control over structure is not equivalent to great art, and a perception of a structure is merely an assistance in coming to understand an author's position. Though the imagery here also contributes to a comprehension of the characters, Penny and Neil particularly are not thereby brought full to life. Though the imagery assists in the evocation of mood, the quality of the prose tends to shift the reader's attention from the climax to the more sensational event which precedes it. In spite of its flaws, however, *Barometer Rising* contains some excellent dramatic narrative; it demonstrates an accomplished incorporation of a political idea and a humanitarian principle into a fictional form, and it retains its importance as a landmark in the development of fictional technique in Canadian literature.

NOTES

1. See Hugo McPherson, Introduction to Hugh MacLennan, *Barometer Rising* (Toronto: McClelland and Stewart, 1958), pp. ix-xv. Cf. Paul Goetsch, "Too Long to the Courtly Muses," *Canadian Literature*, No. 10 (Autumn, 1961), pp. 19-21; Hermann Boeschenstein, "Hugh MacLenna, ein kanadishcher Romancier," *Zeitschrift für Anglistick und Amerikanistik*, 8 (1960), pp. 117-20; and R.E. Watters, "Hugh MacLennan and the Canadian Character," *As a man thinks . . . ed.* Edmund Morrison and William Robbins (Toronto: Gage, 1957), pp. 228-43.

2. This and all subsequent quotations are taken from Hugh MacLennan, *Barometer Rising* (Toronto: McClelland and Stewart, 1958).

3. Cf. George Woodcock, "A Nation's Odyssey," *Canadian Literature,* No. 10 (Autumn, 1961), p. 11.

4. There is perhaps some need to clarify the nature of the meteorological occurrence that is being described. Much stormy weather in the middle latitudes is associated with areas of low barometric pressure, and much fair weather with areas of high pressure. The Bjerknes theory of polar fronts explains the formation of low pressure areas in the northern hemisphere as the counterclockwise pivoting action that is begun when a cold northern high pressure area meets and interacts with a moist southern high pressure area. The air current action of rising and cooling then causes precipitation, and squalls continue until the front is occluded or dispersed, at which time the barometric pressure rises again and more stable conditions ensue.

THE WANDERER IN *BAROMETER RISING*

KATHLEEN O' DONNELL

Hugh MacLennan's novel opens with the statement that "there is yet no tradition of Canadian literature" and proceeds to offer a creative vision of the Canadian environment and character. Dealing with the subject of a returned Canadian soldier in 1917, the author conveys his idea of the special attraction of this nation, and of the traits peculiar to its people.

Neil Macrae is portrayed as the wanderer returned to his homeland. He had been walking around Halifax all day, as though by moving through familiar streets he could test whether he belonged here and had at last reached home.[1] He is motivated by a search for his own identity, the identity of his country, and the relationship between the two. To know himself, to reveal himself, and to be judged truthfully are his urgent desires.

Comparisons with literary analogues help to elucidate the distinctiveness of the Canadian figure. Odysseus is most obviously suggested. Slight biblical allusions remind the reader of the traditional wanderings of Cain. Furthermore, Coleridge's Ancient Mariner is brought to mind for Neil Macrae must speak of and clarify what he has done. The plot of the novel, centering upon the Halifax explosion of 1917, aids the revelation of Neil Macrae as the type of Canadian wanderer. His very name, by its etymology, and the title of the book suggest the power, heritage, and optimism of this figure. The name "Neil" signifies courage. The image in the title is one of hopefulness.

MacLennan's wanderer is one of those who did not die in Flanders. His survival is suspected to be the result of his refusing to obey an order to advance. Macrae, having returned to Halifax, searches for Alec MacKenzie, who alone can supply the evidence which will vindicate him. Actually, the evidence is finally given, in written form

"The Wanderer in *Barometer Rising*," by Kathleen O'Donnell. In *University of Windsor Review*, 3 (Spring, 1968), pp. 12-18. By permission of the author.

and before witnesses. But Neil Macrae, as he develops, overcomes the need for this type of vindication and finally has no interest in it. Truth to self has primacy over proof to others.

This and other relationships in the novel offer revelations of the character and values of the hero. His respect for Alec MacKenzie is partly personal, but is also a mark of his deference for the work and background of the Nova Scotian, who stands as a symbol of the old attitude to work and craftsmanship. Like Neil Macrae's own father, Alec is a representative of the old ideal of individuality and personality in work. This value is one of the objects of Neil's quest. At the end of the novel, it is remarked of him that "he would fight indefinitely to achieve a human significance in an age where the products of human ingenuity make mockery of the men who had created them" (p. 216).

The portrait of Neil Macrae is at first one of physical degeneration. The results of a war injury and shell-shock combine to undermine his health severely. There is "a nervous tic in his left cheek and a permanent tension in the expression of his eyes"; he moves "with jerky nervousness that indicated he was not yet accustomed to his limping left leg" (p. 3); and he is oppressed by "alternate fits of nervous activity and dull apathy" (p. 47). Neil's development through the novel shows him gaining more and more control of both his physical and his mental states. He gains this control through a process of seizing upon the occasions for communication and action, and then of courageously entering into them.

At first, his sickness was to death. This is his thought in his loneliness. "He might as well be dead as the way he was since the chief loss in death was the ability to communicate" (p. 45). Through chance encounters with a talkative restaurant man, then with a former colleague to whom he lies about himself, Neil struggles to conceal his identity. Only the crisis of the explosion and the opportunity which it gives him to lose himself in the service of others supply for Neil an occasion for the display of his true moral grandeur. He struggles to achieve his dignity as a basis for communication, from this he advances to love and the acceptance of responsibility.

His search and his return are for Penelope. On the first day, standing before her house, he could not find the strength to approach her, although it "would be so easy." The author describes Neil's feelings: "Just a few movements and it would be done, and then whatever else he might feel, this loneliness which welled inside like a salt spring would disappear" (p. 8). But Neil was unable to approach her and "turned back down the hill." Penelope had been approached by another suitor, but this was not what Neil feared or even thought of. It was his way to examine himself rather than to examine the situation. And at this point, believing in the necessity for objective vindication, he found himself unworthy to approach her.

A study of the character of Neil demands an examination of Penelope, the mother of Neil's child. She had not married him because of the expected opposition from her father, Geoffrey Wain. Anxiously and fearfully, she had been hoping for the survival and return of Neil. Penelope is the figure of woman alone, persisting in work in order to keep herself in a continual state of fatigue and so escape thinking about her life. For the work itself, she has no false respect. It was the "product of Neil's brain and her patience" which would be "the most uncomfortable craft in the Royal Navy" (p. 20). She examines and judges her life realistically. "She had gone through a ridiculous life during these past few years, trying to outwit the Almighty by handing over her daughter to a kindly uncle and aunt, pretending that her sole ambition was to succeed in a man's profession." Work is an anaesthetic but not powerful enough to overcome completely her loneliness and sense of loss or to obliterate her dream of "herself growing old gently, with children about her, the land where she had been born mellowing slowly into maturity" (p. 14).

No more than Neil, does Penelope see fate as the cause of her unhappiness. With greater truth than he, she takes the responsibility for having shaped the outcome of her life. "And yet she knew that her earlier life had never been especially contented, nor were the things on which she had spent her time calculated to induce any such picture as the one which now filled her mind" (pp. 14-15). Yet there is uncertainty in Penny's thought. She admits that she had not planned a way of life that would lead to a gentle and happy old age, but yet she feels that to have planned such a life would have been impossible in her time and place. Now in recognizing the power of circumstance, "She quivered at the thought of how helpless her existence had been in the current of forces she had been able neither to predict nor to control" (p. 15). Penelope is fondest of her Aunt Mary who appears as "a woman who has spent a lifetime in moderate defiance of her environment" (p. 23). And so Penelope escapes the uncertainty through work "to avoid thinking too deeply about matters she could not control" (p. 20).

The name "Penelope" means "weaver." True to her name, this Penelope waits patiently, continuing her work until Neil returns. It is only he who can awaken her to the fullness and beauty of life. He returns to save her from "the habit of restraint, the cold control she had trained herself to acquire" (p. 219).

Neil never weakens in his purpose to vindicate himself and so regain an honourable life in Canada. In spite of all the coincidences and unexpected circumstances, he will not admit that they have power to determine the direction of human lives. "Even though his world was composed now of nothing but chance, it was unreasonable to believe that a series of accidents should ultimately matter' (p. 7). Later, in discussing with Alec MacKenzie the crucial day on which he had defied the order, Neil reflects on the power of all the diverse circumstances in affecting the rest of his life, and tries "to resist the conviction that chance and preposterous accident had complete control of a man's life" (p. 134). The peculiarity of Neil's thought is that it is totally negative. That chance is not ultimately meaningful, he believes; that what is ultimately meaningful, he does not know.

At first, fear dominates Neil. He fears to be recognized before he is vindicated. He fears to meet any of his army companions. This fear causes him to lie about himself and his actions. It is overcome under the influence of the explosion, which Neil thinks of as "a devastation more appalling than anything he had witnessed in France" (p. 161). The physical danger has little effect on the hero. It does not cause him to panic. Rather it provided the occasion by which he escaped self, and lost fear in love. The author comments: "It was only then that he realized he no longer cared who recognized him.

Even though he was still subject to court-martial, his personal danger ceased to matter" (p. 166). In the following episodes, Neil exhibits bravery, generosity, strength of mind and body such as lead us to respect him and to believe him to have been equally capable of brave acts on the battlefield.

Geoffrey Wain remarks on fear: "I'm afraid I don't believe [sic] the ordinary man is capable of real courage. He's afraid all the time, particularly of his neighbour's opinion. That's the main thing that gets him into the army and keeps him there. When another sort of fear becomes stronger than that one, he panics" (pp. 29-30). His remarks on others are actually comments on himself, as is revealed in the description of his reaction to the battlefield where men under his command lay dead or severely attacked. At that time Wain's "anger disappeared and his fright amounted to panic. He had visions of dismissal for incompetence" (p. 133).

Wain lacks the self-control and will power that belong to Neil. By the circumstances of their lives, enmities have developed between the two. Neil is the son of Wain's sister who died at his birth and for whose death Wain unreasonably holds him responsible. This unreasonableness of Wain is signified in the recurring image of the sloven or wain wildly careening through city streets (pp. 6, 81). The plunging horses pulling the wagon out of its true course are analogous to Wain's passions exerting their force over the man. The image of Wain in death naked beside his mistress is the author's comment on his life. Thereafter occurs Murray's vision of the wain in control and good use: "He saw green trees under the sun and heard locusts shrilling at high noon and there was no more snow because it was midsummer; and hay wains were coming up the hill and after sunset the sea-run salmon would be rising in the river" (p. 212).

It is the thought of home that raises Neil's spirits and gives him "an unexpected wave of exultation." He expressed this value more emotionally than intellectually. "He had forgotten how it was, but now he was back, and to be able to remain was worth risking everything" (p. 4). Neil is dedicated to the purpose of finding a way to stay in Canada where he had been born. All his emotions are reduced to the simple desire for an acknowledged right to exist here

(p. 79). The desire to preserve life is instinctive, though not logical, for the future gave no promise of being superior to the past. The author amplifies: "It was his future, and that was all he could say of it. At the moment it was all he had" (p. 7). He is so certain in this homeland instinct that he is absolutely unperturbed by Murray's message from Wain: "If you don't get out of Canada immediately, he says he'll prosecute you to the limit" (p. 116). To this threat, Neil laughs.

Neil wanders as if he is guilty and therefore unworthy to return to his foster father's house. Like the prodigal son who had left his father's protection, Neil comes to know the poverty, the shoddiness of the world: "plastered walls, sticks of furniture that looked like rubbish, everything greasy and hand-touched, sour smells issuing into the streets" (p. 89). All his senses are assailed with the offensive sights, smells, sounds, which he had never known because he had always avoided the North End.

The action of the novel takes place in early December. It is, in Christian thought, the time of waiting. It was the time when "the winter snow had not yet fallen and the thin soil had frozen onto the rocks, the trees were bare and the grass was like straw, and the land itself had given up most of its colour" (p. 3). The Christian allusions are rare, and are mostly clustered in the scene of the drunken Angus Murray in the whorehouse. He there states that he has seen a man risen from the dead (p. 137). Easter imagery is suggested again after the explosion when Neil reflects: "There had been one splendid, full-throated bellow of power: the earth had trembled, houses fallen, fires arisen" (p. 197). Out of this disruption arose the new Neil, the man who overcame fear with love.

References to types of wanderers in classical, biblical and English literature are meant to clarify our understanding of the Canadian figure. In this fiction, he is revealed as courageous in war, loyal in love, steadfast in his cause, clear-sighted in evaluating persons and their work. Most remarkable are his love of country and his spontaneous dedication to the afflicted. The distinctiveness is not named. It is implied throughout the novel as consisting of the qualities of love, patriotism, truth. MacLennan uses only the word "something."

"Merely to have been born on the western side of the ocean gave a man something for which the traditions of the Old World could never compensate" (p. 4).

The Canadian wanderer returned is like the Anglo-Saxon wanderer for whom exile was the great wretchedness. Both are without bitterness and without fear. MacLennan describes, through his character Murray, a childlike longing for the familiar. "So, like the wanderer, the sun gone down, darkness be over me, my rest a stone—that's your Nova Scotian, if you've the eye to see it. Wanderers. Looking all over the continent for a future. But they always come back" (p. 136).

It is only by knowing himself as a wanderer that Neil Macrae gains peace. Only once and briefly is peace suggested in reference to Neil. It is achieved symbolically in the Wanderers' Grounds. "His muscles were tired with long walking, but the strange sense of peace grew as he watched the sun roll over the line of trees by the Wanderers' Grounds and disappear in fire" (p. 78). In the physical wandering of Neil and the intellectual wandering of Angus Murray, MacLennan draws a picture of the Canadian as explorer-wanderer who always returns home. The thought is expressed in the "thinking reed" image by which Murray defined himself (p. 189).

The end and object of all Neil's wandering is Canada. The meaning attached to this nation can be understood through the accumulated images of an arc or arch. First, confusion is signified in the whiplash arched across the plunging horses of the racing slovens: "and the lash flicked in a quick cracking arc over the sidewalk" (p. 6). Then there is the Roman arch of Wain's warehouse revealing his material stability and power (p. 57). The image evolves through MacLennan's description of the "bluish flicker of arc-lamps" (p. 123), in the Halifax night. The climax of these images is reached in Neil's vision of Canada as an arch of unity and communication. "But if there were enough Canadians like himself, half-American and half-English, then the day was inevitable when the halves would join and his country would become the central arch which united the new order" (p. 218).

Walking in the Public Gardens, Neil delineated his feeling of attachment to and ownership of the country. He felt, "That Halifax for all its shabbiness was a good place to call his home." The author says: "It was a heritage he had no intention of losing" (p. 79). This is the inheritance of nature, the great richness, variety, and beauty of land and water in a country that can experience simultaneously the darkness of Nova Scotia and the British Columbian noon with all the intervening shades over city and river, prairie and mountain.

> The sun had rolled on beyond Nova Scotia into the west. Now it was setting over Montreal and sending the shadow of the mountain deep into the valleys of Sherbrooke Street and Peel; it was turning the frozen St. Lawrence crimson and lining it with the blue shadows of the trees and buildings along its banks. . . . Now the prairies were endless plains of glittering, bluish snow. . . . Now in the Rockies the peaks were gleaming obelisks in the mid afternoon (p. 79).

NOTE

1. *Barometer Rising* (Toronto, 1941), p. 1. All subsequent references are to this edition.

TWO SOLITUDES

I. M. S.

Hugh MacLennan, we are told, is "the most talked about author in Canada today." *Two Solitudes* and *Barometer Rising* have had large sales. Further, the general tone of comment on *Two Solitudes* has been most favourable: 'modern', 'timely', 'brilliant', 'a major novel' may be listed as typical words of praise. But there have been a few discordant notes in the conventional paean. In some easily overlooked paragraph, an occasional reviewer has felt compelled to refer to it as "over coarse."

This disparagement is noteworthy. Our book reviewers during the past fifteen or twenty years have been chary about pointing out such characteristics. There has been a fear that such strictures might smack of what Dr. Rhodenizer in his handbook on *Canadian Literature* (1930) regards as the "vicious prudery" prevalent in Canada, and many artistic authorities have written as if social hypocrisy were the chief swaddling-band confining our fiction writers to provincialism and mediocrity. Perhaps *Two Solitudes* may mark a milestone in the shifting of emphasis on this question. Henceforth the artistic cohorts may relax. They have won their victory. Puritanism has been completely outgrown, or authoritatively silenced. *Two Solitudes* might be said, almost, to have made clear the way for a Canadian *Forever Amber*, should anyone care to harvest another such crop. And Canadian criticism, now that fiction has clearly established its prerogatives, may likewise reserve to itself some few rights.

At first survey *Two Solitudes* seems to approach the possibliity of greatness. The author has chosen an ambitious theme, the difficulties in Canada caused by the two old strains in our population differing in religion and education. And further he has been ambitious to work it out in terms described by his character Paul: "I don't seem able to look at politics as if it were a science. I look at

Review of *Two Solitudes,* by I. M. S. In *Queen's Quarterly,* 52 (1945), pp. 494-96.

people instead." Such should be the very stuff of a fine novel. Besides, Mr. MacLennan lives in Montreal and the Eastern townships and must therefore possess intimate knowledge of many types of men in his chosen social field. That his endeavour has achieved no small success and has created a picture of his time which proves interesting and concrete, his sales amply prove.

And yet *Two Solitudes* is a disappointing book. Not so much because the picture is biased and unfair, but because it has so little of the illusion of reality in either its atmosphere or its character-drawing. It is the work of a writer familiar with the surface newspaper literature on the subject, rather than with the people themselves, their minds and their hearts. The author is too aloof from the characters. Their problems are an academic study and the irony of caricature becomes for him and for us the most real and entertaining bond of union with them. For example, the funeral of Sir Rupert Irons is the most alive episode in the book, and it is based wholly on sarcasm. The preparations for the death of M. Tallard make but a journalist's report in comparison. It is, of course, a virtue for an author to be objective, but he must seek objectiveness in treatment, not remoteness from life itself.

It is this remoteness from life, supplemented by a desire to make his page vivid through his good gift for observing details, that leads Mr. MacLennan into his most glaring and irritating absurdities. Unfortunately there is not space to quote full examples, but a brief one may be included and others indicated. Janet Methuen has received at the village post office the government notice of the death of her soldier-husband overseas. She is stunned, but rallies her forces and turns to walk home. A cart passes her on the road and we are told: "She was unaware of the farmer standing in the front of it, holding the reins." So far not too false a note, although one questions the mention of the farmer holding his reins. He in no way helps us to understand Mrs. Methuen's subjection to her grief. The next line betrays the cold, academic indifference of her maker as he constructs her story, not from understanding and insight, but from some strange idea of what realistic writing demands. He continues thus: "The tobacco stains on his [the farmer's] heavy mustache were orange in the eerie light. His cart held a load of steaming manure."

If we continue with Janet a little longer, we hear her father, Captain Yardley, tell a tale to M. and Mme. Tallard, who happen to be visiting him. It is a coarse story which not even a barnyard stable-boy would have thought of telling in such company. And Captain Yardley, although drawn as a diamond emphatically in the rough, is still represented as a diamond, and with an innate gentleness towards women and children. But here again, his unreflecting creator decides that he must be adding to the truth of his picture whenever he superimposes something of the earth, earthy, upon his page. Another instance may be indicated where he interpolates a whole chapter of this kind which, even the most kindly criticism must admit, does nothing but clog his story. Every point this chapter makes about Kathleen has already been suggested. Again, the love of Paul for Heather holds the ingredients of a pleasant love story, but if the account of their first embrace satisfies the author's artistic criterion, his failure to write a great novel needs no further explanation.

Meredith has a saying about "a good wind of laughter" blowing through a book. If there could only have been an occasional breath of such a wind in *Two Solitudes*.

WHERE TWO CIVILIZATIONS MEET
MERRILL DENISON

Currently two Canadian novels are on best seller lists: Mazo de la Roche's *The Building of Jalna*, and Gwethalyn Graham's *Earth and High Heaven*. This reviewer unhesitatingly nominates a third: Hugh MacLennan's *Two Solitudes*, which treats with authority and mature craftsmanship of the seemingly hopeless differences between the two major Canadian peoples, the English speaking and the French speaking or the Canadians and *les Canadiens*.

In scope, design, and execution the MacLennan book is probably one of the most important books yet to come out of Canada—and the qualification is really pure cowardice. If there has been any more important I haven't happened to come across it and I read quite a lot. One can make that statement without casting aspersions on the other two books mentioned. Miss de la Roche's beloved tales of Jalna have dealt with a highly romanticized Canada; Miss Graham's altogether admirable study of anti-Semitism in Montreal is limited in its scope and locale. Mr. MacLennan has chosen to wrestle bare-handed with the problem that is at the very core of Canada's future as a nation and has come off victorious. He has produced a work of major stature.

In any case the presence on American bookstalls of three books of such caliber by Canadians simultaneously is in itself a literary event worth noting. The Dominion has already given us our best Lincoln in Raymond Massey, Woodrow Wilson in Alexander Knox, our sweetheart in Mary Pickford, our biggest income-tax payer in Louis B. Mayer, and our favourite comedienne in Bea Lillie. The time seems to have arrived when she will give us of herself in books.

Two Solitudes is a very penetrating study of that part of Quebec Province where the two civilizations, Anglo-American and Latin-

"Where Two Civilizations Meet" [Review of *Two Solitudes*], by Merrill Denison. In *Saturday Review of Literature*, 28 (March 10, 1945), pp. 13-14.

American, meet and fail to mingle: the Island of Montreal and the adjacent countryside. The period covered extends roughly between the two wars, to be exact from the conscription crisis of 1917 and 1918 to Canada's independent declaration of war in September 1939. The story concerns the two principal groups which contribute to the baffling dilemma of French Canada: one represented by the aristocratic Athanase Tallard and his family, whose forebears sailed up the St. Lawrence with Champlain; the other by the Methuen family of Montreal depicting the Scots-Canadian financial oligarchy which controls the economic destinies of Quebec as well as most of the rest of Canada. Linking the incompatibles together is a kind of Canadian neutral, a retired Nova Scotia sea captain, wise and tolerant, whose daughter, Janet, has married into the Methuen tribe and who buys a farm near the once seigniorial acres of Tallard to be near her.

Because the French side of the Canadian picture is by no means as simple as is generally imagined, Mr. MacLennan has equipped the elder Tallard with an ingeniously differentiated family which includes sons of two marriages, Marius and Paul, and an Irish-Canadian Catholic wife, the attractive and beddable Kathleen. The devoutly religious Marius, warped by his father's second marriage, is typical of the French Canadian youth which hates *les Anglais*, whether they be Canadian, British, or American; Paul, of the type which is at home in either language and either culture; Kathleen, whose instincts are generous and whose perceptions sensory, of a wider human group to whom racial and political antagonisms mean very little.

Athanase himself belongs in still another class: that of the cultured French Canadian with a European education and no business instincts whatever. He is a Member of Parliament and his library contains the works of Rousseau and Voltaire but no image of the Virgin or the Christ, a fact which sharpens a natural antagonism between himself and Father Beaubien, the parish priest. However, the inevitable clash between the two does not reach its climax until Athanase, quite inadvertently, interests one of the Methuen hierarchy, McQueen, in the river which tumbles down off the Laurentian Shield near Saint-Marc-des-Erables. McQueen decides to develop the waterpower and establish a textile factory and in the struggle that follows between Athanase and the priest both go down. Athanase first loses to the priest and then McQueen, and the priest loses to the bishop. The falls are made to run down a tube, the factory is built, and the rural parish with its pre-Conquest Norman flavor becomes one of the industrial towns which are altering the texture of Quebec life.

Obviously, Mr. MacLennan was interested in creating a structure upon which he could present almost all phases of French-Canadian life. This he has succeeded in doing with great truth and fidelity. His people are real, human, and authentic. So is his Quebec landscape with its two dominating features: the great river that drains a quarter of the continent and the blue Laurentian Hills that recede north to the frozen reaches of the Arctic. Go north to the St. Lawrence tomorrow and you will find them just as Hugh MacLennan has written about them; the people and their river and their hills. Happily for Quebec's tourist industry you will find other people, too; people who manage to laugh easily and often, and who, on occasion, can be pretty good fun to be with—but Mr. MacLennan was writing about another family.

The same observations hold good for his handling of the other side of the picture, the Montreal or English-speaking side. All of it is true, although I have a feeling that when he moves into the urban atmosphere his reporting becomes somewhat more mordant and perhaps with reason. Of course, to any reader unacquainted with the Brahminism of Montreal, its recorded stuffiness, complacency, and arrogance will seem entirely unbelievable. Nevertheless, it is there. It exists—along the grey granite cavern of St. James Street and in the baronial keeps that climb the slopes of Mount Royal. Samuel Butler noted it when he wrote, "Oh, God, Oh, Montreal! " Mr. Mac-Lennan, with his Scots-Nova Scotian background and broadening years at Oxford and Princeton, would, I suspect, be willing to trade one of Butler's "Ohs" for a "damn," and this reaction is by no means unique among sensitive Canadians. In *Earth and High Heaven*, for instance, Gwethalyn Graham deals with much the same people in much the same setting and comes up with much the same picture.

But there is another Montreal, Latin, gay, congenial, the one metropolis on the continent that never stooped to legalize prohibition. And there are more facets to the contacts between the

Canadians and *les Canadiens* than Mr. MacLennan has depicted, and more kinds of Canadians and *Canadiens*. However, there is nothing quite so stupid in a book review, nor more infuriating to an author, than to complain because it isn't a different book. *Two Solitudes* tells a first-rate story in an accomplished and adult manner and, perhaps more importantly at the present time, presents a sincere and unprejudiced picture of Canada's great internal conflict.

For my own part, I am sorry the story does not continue further so that we might get a glimpse of the village of Saint-Marc in the present war. I would like to know what is happening among the Catholic Federation of workers, the Trades and Labour Council, the CIO and CCF. I would like to know what has happened to Drummond's genial habitant, Jean B'tiste, since he became something very different: the French Canadian worker. It is in that change that the developing drama of Quebec now seems to lie.

EACH MAN'S SON

JOYCE MARSHALL

This fourth of MacLennan's novels has two protagonists. One is Daniel Ainslie, a brilliant doctor practising in a Cape Breton colliery town in 1913. The other is Calvinism, or more explicitly the guilt inherent in the mere fact of being alive which is its cramped and bitter offspring.

In Ainslie, MacLennan has come closer than ever before to giving us a character in the round. Intellectually an Agnostic, but at the same time "surer of his fingers than of his soul," Ainslie is ridden by the sense of guilt which is his, half by precept, half by inheritance. He is haunted by what he feels is the failure of his marriage, the fables of his childhood having made it impossible for him to give himself freely to sexual love. He longs for the son he will never have and, when he seems to have found this son ready-made in a gifted boy whose prizefighter father has abandoned him, he is aware, though not always with conscious verbalization, that he is guilty once again in his failure to consider the claims and feelings of the two women involved, the boy's gentle girl-mother and his own wife, and that what he really seeks is not a son but a second self, whom he will miraculously enable to grow up free of the Calvinist myths which have crippled his own life.

We know a great deal about Ainslie, by the time the story has reached the shocking scene which is its climax. We never fail to perceive in what direction he is driven or to recognize the force that drives him. If the author had allowed the man's fears and his always haunting, sometimes immobilizing, sense of guilt to come entirely from his own consciousness, the man might haved lived and moved. But dealing, as he must do, in verbal terms with what is frequently nonverbal material, MacLennan is too persistent in his comments and explanations. He even, and most regrettably, analyses

Review of *Each Man's Son*, by Joyce Marshall. In *Canadian Forum*, 31 (Sep., 1951), p. 140. By permission of *Canadian Forum*.

Ainslie's dilemma for us in his three-page author's note, in so explicit a fashion as almost to make the book unnecessary. Ainslie has enough of the fabric of life in him to have done without this, and his vitality, and our own interest in him, tends to sag under too much external analysis.

As well as this central figure, the author has given us some evocative descriptive material about Cape Breton, a number of briefly sketched Highlanders who, though amusing and seemingly authentic enough, incline toward that definition of *character* which requires the word to be set between inverted commas, some excellent and moving scenes in the decline and fall of the prizefighter, Archie MacNeil, a thin precocious child, and two women—Ainslie's wife, Margaret, and Mollie, the boy's mother—of whom in the final analysis we know nothing. Though they are painstakingly described to us, even to the fine wrinkles about the eyes, each remains in her own way a set of characteristics, a vague figure rising to speak in her turn and sinking again into the mist.

MacLennan has chosen a theme of interest and power, and incidents that climb steadily to a culmination of almost melodramatic horror. But the book remains a theatre in which human figures are moved by ideas, inexorably and sometimes savagely, and though the fusion between these figures and ideas is a little more complete than in any of the author's three previous novels, it still fails to be absolute. Ultimately, Calvinism must remain the true hero of the book.

EACH MAN'S SON

GEORGE WOODCOCK

Each Man's Son, like two of Hugh MacLennan's three previous novels, belongs to that borderland of our father's generation where the subject is neither contemporary nor sufficiently distant to be classed as historical. The world of which it talks, the problems of personal and social adjustment of which it treats, are still too near and personal to the reader for them to have slipped into the easy, dispassionate perspective of the total past. This mingling of the near and the already irrevocably lost confronts the novelist who chooses such a subject with an acute problem of architectural proportion, of modulating his emphases in dealing with a time towards which his— and our—reactions are inevitably unstable. It is no accident that in assessing the past the period immediately preceding our own is always the most neglected and derided, and to attempt to write of his father's days otherwise than in caricature a novelist must either be very courageous or very simple-hearted.

MacLennan, I think, is rather the latter, but it has not entirely saved him from the dangers I have already indicated. It is perhaps a little unfair to use anything out of the *blurb* of a novel in criticising the book itself, yet I cannot help feeling that there is something peculiarly significant in some of MacLennan's own words which the publisher has quoted, presumably with the author's approval. He remarks: "When a novel is finished you can tell if it is good by the way you feel. You wake up in the morning with the sense that the world is new and that you must start all over again learning how to live." Such words can be said by a man of sensibility; they could never be said by a critical man, and it is the critical sense which gives natural balance and the force of contrast to any book.

Review of *Each Man's Son*, by George Woodcock. In *Northern Review*, 5 (October-November, 1951), pp. 40-42. By permission of the author.

MacLennan's plot is built around a small mining community of Highland Scots on Cape Breton Island—the country to which he himself belongs. A miner, Archie MacNeil, has left his home to become a prize fighter in the States, and his wife, Mollie, is left alone to bring up their son. The local doctor, Ainslie, a brilliant surgeon suffering from the frustration of hard routine work in a mining village, is also involved in an emotional conflict with his wife which arises largely out of their inability to have children. He encounters the boy, Alan, and, realising his potential gifts, begins to take an interest in him, to educate him, until the child rapidly assumes in his mind the position of the son he himself cannot produce. His hopes, however, are frustrated when Mollie, fearing that the influence of the doctor will alienate Alan from her, refuses to consent to a continuation of the education plan, and decides to go away with a glib little Frenchman who has settled in the village.

The story now mounts almost neatly into tragedy. Archie Mac-Neil, his boxing career ended by failing sight, returns to find the Frenchman making love to Mollie. He kills them both and himself dies from a stroke, while the child sees the whole of the terrifying scene. We are left with the prospect of Dr. Ainslie—now the intervening characters have all been so providentially swept away—at last being able to realize his desire to love and care for the boy who has become his substitute for a son.

This scanty summary cannot do justice to the ambient darkness of Calvinist guilt in which the tragedy is played. Once again, as in his earlier work, MacLennan cannot avoid seeing life at any age running according to the traditional Greek lines, and the mechanics of a classical destiny grind out their pattern too heavily and harshly on the human weakness of his characters, so that the ending of the book seems almost grotesquely artificial and imposed.

Yet it is a novel with many merits. The relationship of classes and persons in this little society, bound by a common faith in its own damnation, are often subtly portrayed, as well as the fear which always seems to overtop hope in the hearts of its people. There are many passages of writing which, if perhaps not so impressive as the best in *Barometer Rising* and *Two Solitudes*, are sensitive and extremely evocative of the life in this area where, as so often in North America, the new life that emerges is shot through with the shadows of the old world from which its creators came. There are, for instance, the fine chapters which describe Archie MacNeil's downfall as a boxer, the last days of a rather childish and fundamentally well-intentioned primitive who has become involved and finally broken by the corrupt and destroying world of commercialized brutality which centres on the boxing ring. And MacLennan seems finally to have assimilated more thoroughly than before in his fiction that preoccupation with the growth of a Canadian consciousness which beforehand was too often stated in abstract and almost chauvinistic terms that make it a kind of literary sore thumb in the salient points of his earlier novels.

Each Man's Son does not, I think, increase MacLennan's stature as a novelist, and it still leaves some of his fundamental problems unresolved—in particular it does not, as I have said, show any minimization of his tendency to wrench the natural development of human relationships into the pattern of a mechanistic fate. Its virtues, I should say, lie in a more felicitous development of character and incident, and in an integration of the whole action of the novel so that, unlike much in *Two Solitudes* and *The Precipice*, one feels that everything here really belongs to a single and rounded whole.

AN ENOCH ARDEN OF THE THIRTIES

WILLIAM DUNLEA

It is a tacit axiom of our day that where anyone has something to say a novel waits to be born. A variety of reasons for this might be cited, the most natural perhaps being the fact that through the novel the largest audience, actual and potential, will be reached. Another reason is the rather prevalent assumption that novelists are the only people who really know life: must they not *be* practically everything both in life and in enlarging it? Thinkers are no longer trusted out of category, and the novelist seems to be the only philosopher our world will tolerate.

Hugh MacLennan is a writer with a philosophy, a sincere observer who writes competently of his native Montreal. Yet in this book he gives no assurance of novelistic skill. It does not appear that Mr. MacLennan is merely eager to be called "a novelist"; he rather would seem to be hypnotized by this amazon who is such a complaisant plunderer of form. She has so long offered herself as the most malleable drudge of all literary work that it is felt she will accommodate every type of mind. She is past violating.

George Stewart, the narrator of *The Watch*, is a radio commentator, whose story harks back to the turbulent Thirties. It starts off as an Enoch Arden yarn, and though this twist is more an embarrassment than a key to the story, it is a key to the nature of the book.

Jerome Martell is a brilliant surgeon and a dominating personality of rebellious instincts who had gone to Spain and joined the Loyalists; according to official files he had wound up being tortured and killed by the Nazis in the big war. In the interim his wife Catherine had married George, who had always loved her.

Catherine's life has been a daily struggle with incurable heart disease, and George, so much the antithesis of Jerome, failed to

---

"An Enoch Arden of the Thirties" [Review of *The Watch that Ends the Night*], by William Dunlea. In *Commonweal*, 70 (1959), pp. 133-34. By permission of Commonweal Publishing Company.

make the most of a chance to marry her when they were young. Flashback: during the Depression George patches out a living as a provincial schoolmaster, and by the time he attains some security Catherine is married to Jerome; but George is accepted as one of the family, and in no time Jerome descries in him a rare political intelligence and recommends him to the CBC. Meanwhile a galaxy of minor characters from pink to vermilion keeps milling on the fringes, trading platitudes which leave no doubt that something is rotten in the establishment. Jerome is the cynosure in all this, and his gravitational pull on the opposite sex is something fearsome. He is not only an uncanny healer but a bit of a mentalist with a spiritual Midas touch: everyone looks at him and understands.

Most of the book and the people in it simply ache with purple loquacity. George is so sacrificing, Catherine radiates a nobility that embraces all humankind, Jerome is so all-seeing—and yet so blind. And poor Norah Blackwell, who can't help herself when her lethal attraction proves too much for Jerome. But Jerome has been reborn, otherwise he could not well return from the dead and restore the living. With a chivalry bordering on the indecent the author has showered upon his heroine every conceivable compensation for her cross; not only is she a raving beauty, it is she who pities, she who is needed, she who is loved.

One chapter, which tells of Jerome's scarred boyhood in the Canadian wilds, stands on its own. Here the author gets a good purchase on drama inherent in all of his material. Elsewhere there are sage and pertinent reflections on the present, the recent but distant past, and the perennial concerns; for the crux of the message is that the human spirit cannot live from moment to moment.

PEOPLE IN THEIR ENVIRONMENT
W. A. DEACON

The gratifying superiority of Hugh MacLennan's fifth novel over any of its four predecessors may be attributed partly to the greater maturity of the writer, partly to the eight-year gap since *Each Man's Son* (1951) giving more time for second thoughts and, probably, considerable rewriting. Less likely is the explanation to be found in luckier choice of subject. One thing is sure; we are faced with a story vaster in geographic scope and in time. Also, and more important, the author is now in complete control of his narrative at all points. He has written a long, complicated story, in which all parts not only fit but are necessary. A remarkable technical point is that the tale starts in the present and all the rest is flashback to the days when the narrator, George Stewart, was a small boy.

The Watch that Ends the Night is basically a story of love and marriage with an Enoch Arden aspect. The terrain is much alive— "In Montreal, between the break-up and the opening of the leaves, robins calling in Dominion Square"; the horror of St. Catherine Street at night haunted by the jobless in the Great Depression; a New Brunswick logging camp; Moncton through the eyes of an orphaned boy of 10 who had never seen a town. Then this:

> In the early October of that year, in the cathedral hush of a
> Quebec Indian summer with the lake drawing into its fiery
> mirror the fire of the maples, it came to me that to be able
> to love the mystery surrounding us is the final and only sanc-
> tion of human existence.

Character is the true heart of a novel and, in *The Watch that Ends the Night*, Mr. MacLennan is particularly happy in his selection of

"People in Their Environment" [Review of *The Watch that Ends the Night*], by William A. Deacon. In *The Globe and Mail* (Toronto, Feb. 14, 1959), p. 16. By permission of the publisher.

contrasting types. There are a good many of them and each stands out clearly, even minor actors in the drama. Among these looms the massive, able, unfettered Dr. Jerome Martell, a brilliant physician with no use for the orthodoxies, who has deep animosity towards the part played in hospital management by rich donors. In one respect Dr. Martell resembles Dr. Norman Bethune, who went to China as an idealistic Communist. Quite similarly, for humanitarian reasons and inspired by Reds, Dr. Martell in the novel left Montreal to throw in his lot with the freedom fighters in the Spanish Revolution of the 1930s.

So we reach yet another aspect of the book—philosophical-political assessment of the left-wing movement that grew out of the Great Depression. This has been a tragic stage in our history. The cause of freedom was at stake in Spain: idealism died in that struggle. Since Franco, it has been power politics with the avowed liberalism of communism turned into the most brutal of dictatorships. The question now is whether freedom can survive.

Mr. MacLennan's strictures against the Western leaders of that period are deserved. His sad summary is:

> What a generation I belonged to, where so many of the successful ones, after trying desperately to hitch their wagons to some great beliefs, ended up believing in nothing but their own cleverness.

But *The Watch that Ends the Night* cannot be written off glibly as a tragedy. It is a fine interpretation of life, with good and bad intermixed, with the strong and clever people involved with the base and stupid ones, which is the normal lot of mankind. Each chapter has its own variety of interest; suspense is maintained and the ending is close to inevitable.

One piece of interpretation is the finest bit of writing this author has ever done. That is the ugly, inhuman existence of the nameless illiterate boy Jerome in the logging camp, followed by the adventures of his escape into the outer world, followed by the child's rescue by an Anglican clergyman and his wife. Never has child psychology been more shrewdly demonstrated. Readers will find sheer delight in this whole episode.

I am always pleased to find an author constantly deepening his understanding as well as improving his technique. But one aspect of the old MacLennan lingers. Not all readers will agree about the merits of all phases of the new novel. Controversy is good for sales; and nothing is surer than that *The Watch that Ends the Night* will be widely discussed. My firm belief is that this author has now reached the plateau; and I shall expect his future books to be written at this high level.

A SENSE OF WONDER PRESERVED AND SHARED

WALTER O'HEARN

A Canadian novelist of increasing stature, Hugh MacLennan has here contrived to write about pain deeply and movingly, without being merely painful. *The Watch that Ends the Night* begins dramatically enough with Dr. Jerome Martell's return from the dead. Jerome is Enoch Arden with a difference. A hero of forgotten undergrounds, his death at Gestapo hands an accepted myth, he comes back to Montreal in search of Catherine, who was his wife. But married to George Stewart in the meantime, Catherine is "living out her death." Doomed by a rheumatic heart, she makes each day an act of grace. Sally, her daughter and Jerome's, has pushed her father into a back chamber of her mind.

Enough said of the plot of Hugh MacLennan's latest and best novel. What is more important is its theme. Yet this lends itself less easily to summary. It concerns, one might say, the plight of the generation who are middle-aged at midcentury, and their redemption—redemption through suffering, if you like. Yet Mr. MacLennan is no more rewriting Bunyan than he is rewriting Tennyson.

The central figure of *The Watch that Ends the Night* is not Jerome, for all that he is a well-realized portrait of a rebel. Nor is it Catherine who makes a quiet nobility out of living. It is George Stewart, the man of average sensuality (and, one is tempted to add, of average intellect) who has the grace to wonder. George is physically awkward and shy. He is often afraid ("I have never felt safe.").

In his teens he parted company with God; he endured a scorching depression and flirted timidly with the Left. At the top of manhood, with the gloss of modest success on him, he has learned to accept life and even the company of the heroic. He has conquered the

"A Sense of Wonder Preserved and Shared" [Review of *The Watch that Ends the Night*], by Walter O'Hearn. In *The New York Times Book Review* (Feb. 15, 1959), pp. 4-5.©1959 by the New York Times Company. Reprinted by permission.

Great Fear, and he has learned that "it is of no importance that God appears indifferent to justice as men understand it. He gave life. He gave it."

Mr. MacLennan has set this novel in Montreal, where he lives, and whose "harsh and angular" beauties he can evoke better than most writers. Some Montrealers are going to open this book tremulously and plunge into the game called identifications. They will be wasting their time. Obviously some of *The Watch that Ends the Night* has been distilled from the writer's experience, but it emerges in new and unrecognizable form.

Although this is a better novel than he has written before, it is a pity he has killed so many other potential books to make it. Martell deserves a novel of his own. Waterloo School, a survival of Canada's colonial phase (where George teaches in the winter of his discontent), is as rich a ground for satire as Waugh's Llanaba Castle (in *Decline and Fall*); MacLennan dismisses it with a casual lick.

Again, granting him his private world, he has a trick of heightening atmosphere which is not the artist's trick so much as the innocent's. It is not so much taking geese for swans as making paper tigers real. But this is the defect of MacLennan's real gift, which is a sense of wonder, marvelously preserved, and the ability to share it.

MacLennan's Rising Sun

Robertson Davies

If you are one of those people who like to discuss the question of what is a Canadian novel, I direct your attention to Hugh Mac-Lennan's latest book, *The Watch that Ends the Night*. It is Canadian, in that it could not have been written by anyone but a Canadian. Its Canadian quality goes far beyond the facts that the setting of the book is Montreal, and that love and understanding for that city are part of the emotional fabric of the work; it is rather that the thinking and feeling which give the book its weight and worth are Canadian. I realize that such a comment asks for justification.

It is generally acknowledged that the work of the best writers of the American South has qualities which set it apart from the writing of other Americans; geography, economics, history and some measure of local character give rise to these differences. I believe that this is also the case with Canadian writers, and especially those from the older part of the country.

We do not think or feel as people do in New England, or the American West; we have, many of us, British sympathies which we are sometimes reluctant to keep, yet afraid to cast away. Our climate sets its mark on us, making some of us moody and introspective in a fashion which is akin to the Scandinavians, or the Russians, and when we dig deep into ourselves we find matters which are very much our own. We are superficially a simple people, but our simplicity is deceptive; the roaring extrovert is only one kind of Canadian, and not any more representative than the nervous, self-concealing one.

For every Canadian who gets into a huff at the bitter tone of Norman Levine's *Canada Made Me*, there is another who can see

"MacLennan's Rising Sun," by Robertson Davies. In *Saturday Night*, 74 (March 28, 1959), pp. 29-31. By permission of the author and the publisher.

the truth which in Levine has turned to gall. For every man who recalls his own childhood in terms of the boys in Ernest Thompson
Seton's *Two Little Savages*, there is another who sees himself in the
worrying, raw-nerved Harold Sondern, in Ralph Allen's *Peace River
Country*. If Canada gets another hundred years in which to present
herself to the world through her books, this aspect of the Canadian
character will become widely known, and will find affectionate
understanding in the rest of the literate world. "Hamlet with the
features of Horatio," said Douglas LePan of the *Coureur de bois;*
never did anyone pack so much insight into the Canadian character
in a single phrase.

In an excellent introduction to the New Canadian Library edition
of *Barometer Rising* Hugo McPherson says that Hugh MacLennan
was a pioneer in exploring Canada's consciousness. He has continued
so since the publication of that book in 1941, and he has received
small thanks for it. Few critics appear to have been aware of what
he was trying to do. Certainly his aim was not the production of
neatly-turned novels which would sell well in the U.S.A.; that would
have been entirely proper work for a craftsman, but MacLennan deserves a better name—he is an artist. A nice book with a Canadian
icing slapped on it can be written, though not easily; a truly Canadian book is quite a different thing.

Hugh MacLennan has not written nice books, but the best books
of which he was capable, and they have not always been easy or
friendly reading. Always there has been that exploration of his own
very Canadian consciousness, which has thrown up boulders of
philosophical disquisition on what might have been the smooth
lawns of his story-telling. He has refused to bury the rocks and roll
the lawns, and has taken the consequences of his decision.

Now, in his fifth book, he has gained a new mastery over the two
strongest elements in his work; the story-teller and the self-explorer
are one. The effect is virtually to double his stature. The Canadian
novel takes a great strike forward.

The story is of a woman greatly loved by two men. Catherine
Carey was the first love of George Stewart, but whereas she was

emotionally precocious, he was not, and so he lost her, and did not find her again until she was the wife of a rising surgeon, Jerome Martell. When Martell left Catherine, in pursuit of an ideal which took him to the Spanish War, George was her mainstay until Martell was reported dead, and then he was able to marry her. He continued to be her mainstay until her death.

The relations among these three are complex, and one indication of the quality of the book is that it is possible for three readers to interpret them in three different ways, and to provide evidence to support each point of view. My own feeling is that the two men give what is best in life to a woman whom I could not really like; Catherine is a fine example of the spiritual vampire, living on the vital force of others. To other readers she may well seem a true heroine—in Jungian terms, the soul of the hero.

Martell may appear to you as a truly great man, or merely as a man who mistakes his own abundant energy for thought; like all such people he is a two-edged sword, bringing fulfilment to some and ruin to others. George Stewart, who is the narrator and who presents himself (as narrators in books so often do) as a poor fish, is the strongest character, with the poorest sense of self-preservation. But it is his intelligence and insight and worth which engage us when we are impatient of the heroics of Martell, and the posturings of Catherine.

It takes a fine novelist, at the top of his form, to create people about whom we can feel, and argue, so strongly. I have talked to people who have read this book and who accept Catherine as the beautiful, rare person George Stewart believes her to be. One man tells me he thinks Martell is of heroic stature—too much so to be real. Yet another complains that the convention of the narrator is strained, because Stewart reports things of which he could not have had any knowledge.

Still another is engrossed by the description of what Canada felt like during the Depression years—an aspect of the novel which is most skilfully brought forward, and kept in focus, for the greater part of the book. Two more are delighted with the descriptions of

Montreal "the subtlest and most intricate city in North America," which is also among the best things MacLennan has done; I hope Montreal appreciates what has been said about it, but it is unlikely that this is so. (Is it true of Canadian cities, as an English friend of mine says of Canadian women, that they become hostile and suspicious when compliments are paid them?)

There will be downright souls, I fear, who will not think this book Canadian in feeling for the strange reason that it is so plainly the work of a man of extensive and subtle intellect. The emotions which it displays are not simple; the existence, side by side, of love and hate for the same woman in the mind of the man who cannot live without her is hard to get into words, and hard for the reader to swallow, if he has no personal experience of the feeling. Those who turn to novels for simple loyalties and happy loves will catch a Tartar in *The Watch that Ends the Night*.

But a literature has no hope of maturity until its writers embark on precisely this task of capturing the subtleties of human feeling and conduct, and revealing them as they are manifested in their countrymen. The people in this book could hardly be anything but Canadians; Catherine might perhaps exist elsewhere in the form MacLennan has given her, but I do not think so; Martell would be most unlikely in the U.S.A.; George Stewart is Canadian through and through. Their plight is a very old one, which has been explored in every mature literature.

MacLennan's triumph lies in working it out in our terms, in one of our own cities. The task has never before been attempted on this scale in the Canadian novel; it has rarely been done so well in any novel in our time. At what personal cost, no critic can know. MacLennan may say, as Whitman said, "Who touches this touches a man."

JEROME MARTELL AND NORMAN BETHUNE

KEIICHI HIRANO

My thesis therefore proceeds as follows:

1) The figure of Jerome Martell is based on life, that is to say, a certain Norman Bethune who actually existed.[1]

2) In order to make Norman Bethune suitable as the central figure of his novel, MacLennan in his own way had to alter him. In this altering, or refining (I would prefer to call it "falsifying") process, an important aspect of MacLennan's works and the basic character of the Canadian reading public are revealed. MacLennan unintentionally shows his unpainted face.

BETHUNE IN JAPAN AND CHINA

If we assume another entry in our small biographical dictionary, Bethune would perhaps come out like this:

> NORMAN BETHUNE (1890-1939) Born in Gravenhurst, Ontario, Canada. After graduating from the University of Toronto takes part in World War I as medical officer. In late 1936 goes to Spain to help the Loyalists and succeeds in setting up the world's first mobile blood-transfusion unit. In 1937 returns to Montreal and sets forth on a six-month fundraising lecture tour. After joining the Communist Party in Toronto leaves for China in January, 1938. Reaches Yenan in March where he meets Mao Tse-tung and becomes medical officer for the 8th Route Army. Dies in East Shansi in November, 1939.
>
> References: Ted Allan & Sidney Gordon, *The Scalpel, The Sword* (Toronto & Boston, 1952); Chou Erh-fu, *Dr. Pai Chuyen* (Peking, 1948).

From "Jerome Martell and Norman Bethune—A Note on Hugh MacLennan's *The Watch that Ends the Night*," by Keiichi Hirano. In *Studies in English Literature*, 44 (1968), English number, pp. 37-59. The introduction of the essay is not reprinted. By permission of the author and the publisher.

It may perhaps be an exaggeration to say that the name of Dr. Norman Bethune is *extremely* well known in Japan, but it is an undeniable fact that he happens to be practically the only Westerner whose name is treated with deep respect and occurs more or less constantly in articles or books published in this country on Mao's China.

He is, for example, given a sympathetic treatment in a recently published travelogue on New China.[2] There is a picture of Bethune at the operating table taken in the late 30s by Wu in an amateur camera magazine.[3] A Japanese translation of his biography by Allan and Gordon came out in 1965 and was given favorable reviews.[4] These are only some of the Japanese examples that come to my mind immediately.

When it comes to publications coming directly out of China, references to him are so frequent that one may even consider him a trademark of a sort. His name occurs at least twice in the Chinese Red Guards' sacred booklet *Quotations from Chairman Mao Tsetung*. The quotations referring to Bethune are taken from Mao's touching funeral oration on the occasion of Bethune's untimely death.[5] His name also occurs frequently in that sensational bestseller (from 1965 to 1966) *The Diary of Wang Chieh*[6] where Bethune is treated as a veritable guiding light.

Thus one may see that though Bethune may not yet be a household word in Japan, as it is in China now, his name is a relatively well-known one. So, to a Japanese reader who happens to read *The Watch that Ends the Night* by MacLennan, Jerome Martell's figure will almost immediately and quite naturally call forth the figure of Dr. Bethune. He will notice the resemblances, but at the same time will find MacLennan's version of Bethune somewhat unpleasant to the taste. I seem, however, to be anticipating.

NORMAN BETHUNE *vs* JEROME MARTELL

I would here like to give my reasons for considering Jerome Martell to be a figure based on Norman Bethune. This, as mentioned before, may be a foolhardy and futile attempt that totally disregards the title-page warning, but MacLennan's strange reticence concerning Norman Bethune should perhaps bear part of the blame.

To the best of my knowledge, not once has MacLennan acknowledged his, or rather Jerome Martell's, indebtedness to Norman Bethune. At least from what MacLennan has written, no direct evidence is available. We shall have to do with circumstantial evidence.

In the latter half of the 1930s Hugh MacLennan taught at Lower Canada College, Montreal. Thus one may infer that he was familiar with the political and social atmosphere of Montreal in the late 1930s. Dr. Bethune who was then a highly respected surgeon at Sacré Coeur Hospital was also one of the most notorious social lions of the town, and just the type to be the topic of cocktail-party conversations. Young MacLennan, who was then working on his *Barometer Rising*, had a feel for social and economical problems (as evinced by *Barometer Rising* which shows a firmer grasp of the ills of society than his later works), and could not have been indifferent to the comet-like movements of the brilliant surgeon—how Bethune joined the Spanish Loyalists, how he came back to raise funds, his departure to China, and so on. One could surmise that the impact he received from Bethune must have deposited deep in MacLennan's subconscious and came to the surface, perhaps unconsciously, when he began working on *The Watch that Ends the Night*.

Apart from such broad conjectures, there are some close resemblances between Norman Bethune as depicted by Allan and Gordon and Jerome Martell as depicted by MacLennan. The resemblances seem to be too close and too numerous to be regarded as purely coincidental. Item by item they are as follows:

(1) *Family background.* Jerome of *The Watch that Ends the Night* is brought up by the Martells, a pious missionary couple. The Martells' forebears were French Huguenots, those French nonconformists who came to eighteenth century Canada by way of Scotland. Norman Bethune, according to the account in *The Scalpel, The Sword*,[7] was born of a pious missionary couple. The family name Bethune is also of French Huguenot origin.

(2) *World War I.* Jerome Martell takes part in World War I and receives a wound in his thigh. He returns from the war to enter McGill University and becomes a doctor. Norman Bethune also takes

part in World War I and is wounded in his left thigh. He re-enters the University of Toronto to become a doctor. (An important difference here is that Jerome Martell kills a number of enemy soldiers in the war, which results in a deep sense of guilt. Thus, the search for compensation becomes one of the motivating forces in *The Watch that Ends the Night*, a figment of MacLennan's imagination, but a device which comes in handy later.)

(3) *Marriage and separation.* The married life of both Jerome Martell and Norman Bethune is not a happy one. In both cases there is an incompatible difference between husband and wife which leads to separation. Catherine who has a heart ailment is presented in the novel as a quiet, almost angel-like woman, and Frances, Norman's wife, is said to have been the shy and retiring type. The husband, in both cases, is outspoken and flamboyant. One difference here is that Jerome Martell deserts his wife, whereas Norman Bethune is deserted by his wife.

(4) *As surgeon.* Both Jerome Martell and Norman Bethune are Montreal surgeons with high international reputation. (As noted before, when MacLennan took up his position as a teacher in a Montreal high school, Bethune was head of the chest surgery department at Montreal's Sacré Coeur Hospital.) Both Martell and Bethune are interested in the socio-economic aspect of diseases. To quote Jerome Martell:

> The place to attack disease is where it starts, and where it starts—a good deal of it—is in economic conditions. Not enough to eat. Not enough of the right food. The slums. The insecurity. The whole damned nineteenth century set-up. . . . [8]

Norman Bethune is known as one of the earliest advocates of socialized medicine in Canada. It was his assertion that TB feeds on poverty. To quote his own words from his biography:

> There is a rich man's tuberculosis and a poor man's tuberculosis. The rich man recovers and the poor man dies. This succinctly expresses the close embrace of economics and pathology. [9]

They are both sympathetic and keep in touch with the various leftist groups of the city. The difference, however, is that while Bethune's sympathy bears such fruit as the Montreal Group for the Security of the People's Health in July, 1936,[10] Jerome Martell's sympathy with the leftist people only seems to get him into trouble. He even gets involved in a free-for-all.

(5) *Characterization*. Norman Bethune is said to have been a man of fiery character. This is how he is described by his biographers:

> Most people who attempted to define him floundered among all the catchwords. He was mad, some said; vain, charming, irresponsible, sensitive, arrogant, a loyal friend, a great surgeon, a showman, a genius, a demanding child—in short, a zigzagging comet of a man flashing in and out of the lives of many people, leaving some enchanted, some disturbed, some grateful, some saddened, some angered, and some exultant, but none untouched.[11]

Nothing could come closer as a description of MacLennan's Jerome Martell. Not a single word need be changed. An astonishing coincidence, one might say. The only, though very important, difference is that on the whole MacLennan's Martell is made out to be more impulsive, and more irrational. But more on this point later.

(6) *The Spanish Civil War*. Both Martell and Bethune are deeply committed to the cause of the Spanish Loyalists. Leaving their highly paid positions behind, they both go to Spain to help the Loyalists in the medical field. After succeeding in setting up mobile surgical units they return to Montreal to help raise funds for the Loyalists. So far the two have trod the same path, but after their return to Canada the two men have to go their separate ways. Jerome Martell goes back to Spain, whereas Norman Bethune heads west for China.

These are some of the points of resemblance anyone, or to be more exact anyone who has read both *The Watch that Ends the Night* and *The Scalpel, The Sword* can see. The resemblances seem to point clearly that MacLennan had Norman Bethune in mind when he was carving the figure of Jerome Martell. The reticence on the part of the author and also of critics may have stemmed from the fact that the resemblance is too obvious. Who needs to have the obvious pointed out? It could be so, though I doubt it. *The Scalpel, The Sword* was published in 1952. Though *The Watch that Ends the Night* came out in 1959, we have the author's word for it that he had been working on this novel for a period of six to eight years.[12] The following conjecture, then, should not be regarded as too far-fetched. It must have been the publication of Bethune's biography in 1952 that induced MacLennan to write his version of Norman Bethune.

To my approach which is yet in its initial stage, I think I can already hear the murmurs of disapproval. They go like this. A character in a novel like Jerome Martell, no matter how close he may resemble an actual person, cannot in the final analysis claim to be more than fictitious. The only reality a fictional character can lay claim to is the reality it has in the context of the novel, which should in its turn be a self-contained microcosm. Whether or to what degree the character diverges from any actual person should not be a matter of primary importance as the writer of this paper is apparently making it out to be. And so on and so forth.

One does not have to be an advocate of any new or old school of criticism to raise such objections. I agree that this type of objection is, in its own limited way, a sensible and a valid one. Nevertheless, I feel strongly that in Jerome Martell, or to be more precise, in the way Norman Bethune has been altered and transformed into Jerome Martell, there is something that we cannot and should not overlook.

To make the point clear, let us consider another case. If, for example, we were using such figures as Hitler or Stalin (in whatever disguised forms) in a work of imagination, would we be completely free to tamper with them? Is a writer, so long as he labels his work "fiction," allowed to depict Hitler as a warmhearted humanitarian, for example? Even a fiction writer does not have that degree of absolute freedom. There must be a responsibility—a pre-literary responsibility, if you like—on the part of the writer. A writer owes it to his society not to be party to any intentional falsification. He is not given unlimited freedom to alter or doctor "life" in order to add to the reality (or beauty or respectability or whatever it is) of his "art."

From the standpoint of literature, or belles-lettres, the ground I am standing on may not be too firm. I am aware that my approach is, to put it mildly, somewhat extra-literary. But with the social responsibility of such influential writers as MacLennan foremost in my mind, I feel that I have to stick to it, at least for the present paper.

To go back to Jerome Martell and Norman Bethune. I have shown that these two resemble each other closely. There are, however, many aspects of the two figures that differ from each other, sometimes subtly and sometimes flagrantly. It goes without saying that the fictional Martell does not have to be a scrupulous imitation of the real Bethune. A writer is entitled to his own interpretation, and Jerome Martell may diverge from Norman Bethune in accordance with MacLennan's interpretation. True. But it is precisely when MacLennan puts in his own interpretations that I feel I have to raise objections. Why? I do not object to the fact that the two differ occasionally, which is perhaps as it should be, but to the way they differ.

To be more specific. I have already mentioned that there is a difference in the way the marriage of Jerome and Catherine and that of Norman and Frances end. In both cases, the partners are diametrically opposed in temperament to each other. "The fiery husband and the icy wife" may sound too much like a mere figure of speech, but there seems to have been something like that in the relations. In the novel, Jerome Martell gets into trouble, gets involved with a nurse, clashes with his superiors, and ends up leaving his wife, whereas in the case of Norman Bethune it is the other way round. The wife deserts the husband.[13] A trivial point, perhaps. But we should note that even this slight deviation is a change for the worse, that is to say, the actual situation is altered so as to make the husband appear worse than he actually was. Or, to take another trivial point. Bethune, who was a generous patron of art,[14] was also known to be quite a good artist himself. In *The Watch that*

Ends the Night, however, this artistic talent which Bethune had is transferred from husband to wife. Catherine is the sensitive artist, a sharp contrast to the rugged brutal husband. To call this a change for the worse may be going a bit too far, but it will perhaps show how consistent MacLennan is in his deviation from the real.

We can put it this way. MacLennan always makes it easier for the readers to judge and to place the blame where it belongs. Faced with a man like Norman Bethune, the readers (and presumably Mac-Lennan) would be at a loss, but with Jerome Martell everything seems to be clear. Between Jerome and Catherine, no one would hesitate to lay the blame on the former. Whether a novel is "popular" or not depends to a large degree on how ready the author is to cater to the tastes and judgments of the reading public. Mac-Lennan somehow seems to be more than ready.

Let us move to more important issues. Compare for example how the two responded to the political issues of the time. As men-tioned before the two resembled each other in the way they could grasp the mutual relationship between disease and economics. But there is a difference. Norman Bethune's interest is based solidly on his own researches and investigations (he even went to the USSR in 1935 to study socialized medicine firsthand), whereas Jerome Mar-tell's is more instinctive and impulsive. The crucial issue, however, is the Spanish Civil War.

As regards the war in Spain, the two seem to be treading the same path. Outwardly they respond in much the same way. The difference in motivation, however, is noteworthy. Norman Bethune realized that such problems as socialized medicine, the rehabilitation of TB patients, and the Spanish Civil War were all interwoven, and therefore not to be tabulated as separate areas of concern.[15] His commitment to medicare and his sympathy for the Spanish Loyalists had the same root, and he was well aware of it. Unlike Jerome Martell, he did not go to Spain on an impulse. In contrast, Jerome Martell's reason for going to Spain is given as follows. He is ex-plaining to George Stewart, the narrator, his case:

> These people [in Montreal] think I'm a Red because I want
> to help the Spanish Loyalists. My God, how stupid can they

be! I'm not a revolutionary. I see a thing that has to be
done—and I do it. . . . How lucky you are, not being born
with my temperament.[16]

With Jerome Martell, helping the Loyalists in Spain is more a
matter of temperament than of principle. In defense of his Spanish
adventure Martell again and again falls back on the irrational. "Can
I help my own vitality?" or "Perhaps you can tell me what there
is to protect a man like me against his own impulses?"[17]

So we see that Jerome Martell went to Spain not because he had
any rational or ideological grasp of the situation but because he
just couldn't protect himself from his impulses. And as if this down-
grading in motives were not enough, MacLennan has to add such
ingredients as Martell's scandalous affair with one of the nurses (she
leaves for Spain on the same ship), and the inevitable clash with his
superiors. The impression the readers get is that even if Jerome
Martell hadn't left of his own free will, people in Montreal simply
wouldn't have tolerated him. He had to leave to get out of hot
water. Thus the readers no longer have to worry about the rights
or wrongs of the Spanish Civil War. Martell's behaviour is made
completely understandable. He could have gone to help the Falang-
ists in Spain as far as MacLennan and the readers are concerned.

Another quotation. This time in connection with Catherine whom
he had deserted.

I don't really think I was running away from her when I went
to Spain. . . . I was running away from myself, not from her.[18]

The fact that Martell had killed a number of enemy soldiers in
WWI and had become a man suffering from a terrible sense of
guilt now comes in handy. He just had to run away from himself.

Creating plausibility (on the popular story level) out of the chaos
of reality—this seems to be MacLennan's forte. There is no reason
to suppose that MacLennan's own view of the Spanish Civil War
was more rational. Through the narrator who serves as the author's
mouthpiece MacLennan lets it be known that he prefers to regard the
Spanish Civil War as a gigantic mystery play, Spain being the stage
on which a multitude of passions met.[19] He mistrusts people (Norman Bethune, for one?) who think there is a rational explanation

for it.[20] Such obscurantism (as I would prefer to call it), when it implies refusal of the facile and the slick, could be one form of integrity. But unfortunately our MacLennan seems to be too much a master of platitudes.[21]

To return to the comparison. Both men, as we have seen, go to Spain to help the Loyalists. The great difference in their motives do not yet show. The big change, or the big flight of imagination on MacLennan's part, comes later. After a stint in Spain, the two men return to Montreal to raise funds. Jerome Martell is already disillusioned about the war, but after an unsuccessful fund-raising campaign returns to Spain. We see him referring to the war as "this whole miserable tragic business."[22] He realizes that he is being used as a tool by the Communists but goes back because he is "a divine fool."[23]

Norman Bethune, after his return to Montreal, treads a different path. He travels throughout the country calling for moral and financial support of the Loyalists. (Unlike Martell's his campaign is said to have been very successful.[24]) One would think that it's about time Bethune got disillusioned, but he refuses to follow the all too familiar pattern—the pattern followed by Koestler, Spender, Orwell, and many others. Instead of becoming disillusioned with communism, Bethune joins the Communist party in Toronto towards the end of 1937. While Jerome Martell, prompted no doubt by his creator, had to declare that he was "not a revolutionary,"[25] Bethune, according to his biographers, never denied the fact that he was a Communist.[26] This is one side of Bethune that not only MacLennan but most Canadians (so it seems) choose to disregard.

Early in 1938, instead of returning to Spain, Bethune leaves for China. The reasons are given clear enough in a letter to his former wife:

> Spain and China are part of the same battle. I am going to China because I feel that is where the need is greatest; that is where I can be most useful.[27]

As it is not my intention in this paper to pronounce a eulogy upon Bethune, I need not go into further details.

Now, what about Jerome Martell? After the Loyalists' defeat in Spain, Martell escapes to France where he is captured by the Nazis, after which he is imprisoned successively in Poland, Russia, and China. He has managed to survive only because he could prove himself useful as a doctor. By now he is totally disillusioned with communism. In China he contracts a disease (note the resemblance to Bethune) and is practically left to die, until one day he wakes up to find Jesus himself in the cell with him.[28] He is alone no more. He has returned to the faith of his Halifax boyhood. A moving scene indeed for the readers. "If only Norman Bethune had been like this!"—MacLennan seems to be saying.

It is a well-known fact that Norman Bethune, contrary to the expectations of his more respectable friends, never became disillusioned. He seems to have had no scruples about working and dying for Mao's 8th Route Army. MacLennan, of course, could not have been ignorant of the fact. The point, therefore, seems to be this. Dr. Bethune was a highly respected man in his Montreal days. That he should have been caught in the political enthusiasm of the late 30s is understandable (who wasn't in those days?), but the fact that he remained enthusiastic, as it were, till his death without once being disillusioned is something that runs against the grain of society—respectable society, that is. There is a limit to what society can stand. MacLennan, in this respect, seems to have a canny feel for the taste of the reading public. He accordingly cuts Bethune down to size. The inscrutable (from the readers' standpoint, that is) course followed by Bethune is transformed into the more understandable and more forgivable course followed by Martell—from political involvement to disillusion, and from disillusion to the final discovery of God. To the Jerome Martell type of wandering, the readers can respond easily. The wild oats he sowed, the agonies he went through, the joy he must have felt at discovering Jesus— these are all understandable. With tears in eyes, and heaving heavy sighs of relief, the readers can follow the story to its happy end.

Norman Bethune as depicted by his biographers does not provide the general reading public with this kind of easy, intimate, and almost comfortable feeling. His life tends to shake us out of our complacency. He even makes us *think*, but who really wants to *think* in this comfortable society of ours? In Bethune's life there are some jarring notes, which as a rule have no place in popular literature. Therefore it behooves a popular writer to muffle and delete these jarring sounds (for the safety of the reading public, presumably), and lo and behold, we have *The Watch that Ends the Night* to replace *The Scalpel, The Sword*—that disturbing, clandestine, and almost seditious work.

EPILOGUE AND CONCLUSION

In January, 1965, a National Film Board documentary of Bethune's life was shown on a CBC-TV special program to mark the 25th anniversary of Bethune's death. Thus Bethune was given public recognition (which does not necessarily mean approval) for the first time since he left the country in 1938. The hour-long program was a moving one, but as far as I remember the emphasis seemed to be on Bethune as a humanitarian. (The script of the documentary film to which I have no access may disprove the impression I received, though I think it unlikely.)

As is usual with such programs, the public response was interesting. Here is how an Ottawa paper referred to Bethune in a review of the film:

> . . . a man who strictly adhered to the basic ethic of his profession—and travelled the world aiding the suffering, no matter who [sic].[29]

The political, or ideological, side of Bethune is completely ignored. For a doctor who heartily believed in communism, we have substituted a Schweitzer-type humanitarian—so noble, but also how safe!

To recapitulate what I have been trying to say. When we compare Jerome Martell as depicted by MacLennan with Norman Bethune as depicted by his biographers, we find that the part of Bethune that goes beyond the reach of social acceptability, or the part that refuses to conform to society's expectations, is cut down and trimmed in an astonishingly consistent way. Jerome Martell, the end product of this consistent chipping, becomes a figure quite pleasing to the taste of the general readers. Despite his forbidding appearance, he is really an easily digestible, absorbable, and hygienically safe food for the public. If this Martell—a Bethune cut down to size—is to be regarded as a man "larger than life," or as a "super-Odysseus," what about the real and actual Bethune? A "supersuper-Odysseus?"

MacLennan in *Barometer Rising* and *Two Solitudes* occasionally showed himself to be a writer perceptive of the ills stemming from our socio-economic system (see his Huntly McQueen). It seems, however, that the more he gained in respectability, and the higher his reputation and status in Canadian society has become, the more respectable his works have become. The occasional social comments he now makes in such periodicals as *Macleans*, though warm-hearted enough, are basically of the type made by George Stewart, that master of platitudes.

Hugh MacLennan is, to the best of my knowledge, one of the most highly regarded men of letters in Canada. Not only the general public but the Establishment (Canada surely must have one) no doubt looks upon him as a wise and extremely reliable (which means "safe") man. There is no fear of his ever rocking the boat. The high respect he enjoys in Canada may be a king-size mess of pottage, but whither his birthright? It seems that he has unconsciously renounced the responsibility that he has as a writer to society. To tell the truth (not what one wants to be the truth), however unpalatable it may be, should be the first and foremost concern of a writer. This, I believe, was Grove's[30] concern when he wrote *The Master of the Mill* (1944). To cater to the tastes of the general public should be the primary concern only of writers of popular fiction.

Jerome Martell, I repeat, is a product made pleasant to the taste of the reading public. I find it difficult to regard him as anything else.

NOTES

1. I am intentionally disregarding the author's (or rather the publisher's) stereotyped warning on the title page, i.e., "The characters and events in this novel are fictitious. Any resemblance to actual persons or events is coincidental ...", a warning too conventionalized for anyone to take seriously.

2. Takeshi Sugimura, *Shin-chūgoku-yūshin* (The Heart of New China) (Tokyo, 1966).

3. *Photo Art* (Kenkōsha, Tokyo), 8 (April, 1966), p. 27. A picture magazine with no political leanings.

4. *Idai naru Shōgai* (The Great Life), tr. by Yūzo Asano (Tōhō-shuppansha, Tokyo, 1965).

5. "In Memory of Norman Bethune" (December 21, 1939), in Mao Tse-tung's *Selected Works*, Vol. II. The quotations show eloquently where Bethune stands in Mao's China. For example: "Comrade Bethune's spirit, his utter devotion to others without any thought of self, was shown in his boundless sense of responsibility in his work and his boundless warm-heartedness towards all comrades and the people. Every Communist must learn from him. . . . We must all learn the spirit of absolute selflessness from him." And again, "What kind of spirit is this that makes a foreigner selflessly adopt the cause of the Chinese people's liberation as his own? It is the spirit of internationalism, the spirit of communism, from which every Chinese Communist must learn. . . ."

6. Wang Chieh is a young soldier who dies while undergoing training in 1965. The Japanese version of the diary is titled *Ohketsu no Nikki* (Tokyo, 1966).

7. The edition the writer has is a Prometheus Book edition (Cameron Associates, New York, 1959). Quotations if necessary will be made from it, the writer having no access to the original Toronto or Boston edition.

8. *The Watch that Ends the Night*, Signet Book (The New American Library, 1960), pp. 151-52.

9. *The Scalpel, The Sword*, p. 67.

10. *Ibid.*, p. 91.

11. *Ibid.*, pp. 70-71

12. MacLennan, "The Story of a Novel," *Masks of Fiction*, ed. A.J.M. Smith, New Canadian Library (Toronto, 1961), p. 37.

13. Technically there was no desertion, but it was Frances who took the initiative. Cf. "Sometimes it would seem to her that she had deserted him, that all would have gone well had she only given him more love." *The Scalpel, The Sword*, p. 71. See also p. 58.

14. The Children's Art School of Montreal which Bethune opened in 1935 was only one of his many pet projects.

15. *The Scalpel, The Sword*, p. 98.

16. *The Watch that Ends the Night*, p. 226.

17. *Ibid.*, p. 253.

18. *Ibid.*, pp. 340-41.

19. *Ibid.*, p. 228.

20. *Ibid.*, p. 271.

21. In a book review of *The Watch that Ends the Night*, Warren Tallman refers to the narrator's penchant for banalities. "Stewart's narration is badly marred by his mania for handing out crashing complacencies on almost every imaginable major consideration in life: marriage, religion, modern love, art, war, sex, neurosis, politics, philisophy, peace, the seasons." See *Canadian Literature*, No. 1 (Summer, 1959), p. 81. One can substitute MacLennan for Stewart with impunity.

22. *The Watch that Ends the Night*, p. 278.

23. *Ibid.*

24. *The Scalpel, The Sword*, p. 163.

25. *The Watch that Ends the Night*, p. 226.

26. *The Scalpel, The Sword*, pp. 165-66. Cf. also "Norman Bethune boasted he was a Communist." (Dr. Richard Brown), *ibid.*, p. 316.

27 *Ibid.*, p. 167.

28. *The Watch that Ends the Night*, p. 308.

29. *The Ottawa Journal* (Jan. 14, 1965).

30. Frederick Phillip Grove (1871-1948). A striking illustration of what *can* happen to a writer of integrity in Canada, and, needless to say, a sharp contrast to MacLennan.

THE RELATION OF STRUCTURE TO THEME IN
THE WATCH THAT ENDS THE NIGHT
W.B. THORNE

The theme of Hugh MacLennan's *The Watch that Ends the Night* rests on an intricate series of correspondences between the structure of the novel, the relationships of the characters, and the first person narrative focus which is used to sew together the correspondences. In a sense the novel has a kind of pyramidal structure in which the base is the Thirties and the Great Depression, the middle level is the triangular relationship between the three main characters, and the zenith is the first person narration of George Stewart, who makes possible the relationship in time between the past and the present and the relation of the central biographies. In him the experiences of the others come to a muted epiphany. Perhaps a clearer indication of the novel's structure is its sociological panorama, in front of which the representative products of the Depression act out their passion play.

The three major figures of the novel discover themselves against the vast panorama of the Thirties, Canadian geography, and the social, political, and economic development of Canada and the Western world, as well as against the panorama of their individual past experience. Correspondences in structure, characterization, and theme are continuously focused in the first person narrative of George. They begin and end in him, and the other two main characters, though they experience their own rebirth, are again reborn in the multiple personality of Everyman George, who has at last learned how to retire meaningfully into himself and "die into life."

To convey the parallel themes of "living your death" and "escape from self," the novel uses the technique of composite biographies

"The Relation of Structure to Theme in *The Watch that Ends the Night*," by W.B. Thorne. In *Humanities Association Bulletin,* 20 (1969), No. 2, pp. 42-45. By permission of the author.

which has recently become commonplace in North American novels. The narrative does not develop chronologically in a straight line; instead it is convoluted so as to accommodate a series of flashbacks which provide insights into past events and illuminate the significance of the present in the life of George Stewart and his semi-invalid wife Catherine. By juxtaposing past and present in the lives of the three main characters, MacLennan is able to establish the influence of the Thirties on the Fifties in Canadian social development, and to delineate a significant continuum through the Everyman function of George Stewart.

The plot therefore is a string of parallel biographies suspended in relief against the social, economic, political and moral background of the Thirties, Forties and Fifties. George's narrative position is used to present the past as it relates to the present, and to explore the development of individuals whose lives may indicate the spectrum of Canadian personality in the era under observation.

The triangular relationship of Jerome, Catherine, and George cannot be dissociated from their independent biographies and the theme of isolation and alienation which runs through most of the novel. Against the panoramic background of the novel, George Stewart, like Canada, comes of age, adopted and guided by his spiritual parents, Catherine and Jerome. In the relationship between these people and others loosely associated with them and their development, a further series of parallels is used to establish their fundamental likeness and their fundamental relationship to the social fabric of Canadian life, which left its indelible imprint upon the restless idealistic products of the Depression years.

In a strange way, George and Jerome are brothers in arms, not only in Catherine's arms, but also in their relationship to the forces of change impinging upon Canadian life. Both are spiritually adopted by people who exerted a tremendous psychological influence upon them. Both finally establish a commitment to something outside themselves and come to a deeper understanding of self and of its relation to external reality, after having first withdrawn from the reality which is too horrifying for them to face.

The structure of the novel is designed in such a way as to support these symbolic resemblances and to focus them in the curious relationship between Jerome, George, and Catherine, a psychological trinity based largely on its ultimate effect upon George himself. To establish the interdependence of areas of experience and of characters, MacLennan constructs his novel in seven related units which explore three biographies. The novel moves backward and forward in time, not only in the experience of a single individual but also in the experience of the whole country and, partially at least, the Western world. Relationships backward in time and laterally in space and significance are complex and far-reaching, for they extend the web of meaning the novelist wishes to convey.

Part One opens in the present, in the autumn of George's life, when Jerome re-enters George's life and stimulates reverie and the flashbacks which explore the youth of George and Catherine. The second section of *The Watch that Ends the Night* moves back in time to explore George's childhood and the psychological forces that retarded his emotional development and his discovery of himself. The central incident of this section is his unconsummated love affair with Catherine Carey, which almost brings him out of himself and into maturity. At a crucial moment, however, the orthodox conservatism of his background becomes militant in the tyrannical person of Aunt Agnes, who intimidates George and destroys for years any possibility of his reaching security and self-confidence. Though George's rebellion is short-lived, Catherine's is intense and successful. Whereas George sinks under the burden of family and the financial ruin of his father, Catherine becomes emancipated through her desperate desire to tear her pleasure through the iron gates of life.

Part Three returns to the present to examine George's confused reaction to the resurrection of Jerome and acts as a transition into the social and political milieu of the pre-war period. The present occupies so little time in the bulk of the novel that the initial sections dealing with it may be described as intercalary units which do little more than sew together the parallel biographies in preparation for the mystical conclusion. For this reason, perhaps, the past has a denser reality than the present in *The Watch that Ends the Night*, and the conclusion has the twilight transparency that George sees in the faces of Catherine and Jerome.

In Part Four MacLennan describes George's flight from reality in such a way as to provide a foil or parallel for Jerome's biography in Part Five. In this section, more than any other in the novel, George is a Canadian Everyman figure, in whose experiences the stultifying impact of the Depression may be implied. George's passion is not intense enough for the neo-religion of Communism to exert the hold over him that it does with Norah Blackwell, Arthur Lazenby, and Jerome; but as George stumbles through the sloughs of despond, he is significantly influenced by the tortured idealism of the Thirties. This section of the novel brings back into his life Catherine, now married to Jerome, and provides for him the emotional support which earlier years have denied him.

Part Five is composed of the brutal and romantic saga of Jerome Martell, fatherless orphan of the logging camps who carries on his shoulders the cross of idealism and the agonizing question of "What is my duty?" Through the focus on Jerome and his animal magnetism, the quiet Canadian stereotype of George is given dimension and, perhaps, by contrast with Martell's heroic nature, more reality. Jerome is developed as a symbol of the alienation, the loneliness and the questioning of the Thirties. Part Five seems, as a result, the key to the structure of the novel and also the integrating unit in the development of the theme which is so closely connected to the structure. Part Six, which carries Jerome's life history into the Thirties and focuses upon the flight from Catherine to Spain, acts as a foil to Part Five and also to the continuum of George's psychological development, which is intimately connected with Jerome's own experiences. The symbolic father-son connection between Jerome and George echoes the novel's contention that the Thirties was the time of the fatherless ones, a time when the centre could no longer hold and the best were full of passionate intensity. This section of the novel illustrates better than any other the delicate correspondence between structure, character relationships, and theme in *The Watch that Ends the Night*. The structural invagination of the novel is necessary to explore the conditioning influence of national experience upon those who learned to live their death and to face life on its own terms, not on the terms of some distorted social or political interpretation of it. This structural pattern also supports significant character parallels and relationships. Parts Five and Six make very clear the scapegoat relationship of Jerome to George. In Part Seven, Jerome heals Catherine, just as Catherine and he together heal George. This return to the present is thoroughly dependent on the novel's conception of the influence of the past and the relation between experience and personality, and between experience and views of reality.

The conception of return from death grows inevitably from the narrative method and structure of *The Watch that Ends the Night* and depends finally upon the juxtaposition of parallel biographies. All three characters, as a result of their individual experiences, have developed a vision of life. George's ultimate insight, however, is somewhat parasitic in nature, just as is Catherine's, in that he has leaned on the superior energy, vitality, and reactions of Catherine and Jerome, who have to some extent mothered and fathered him into maturity. The search for self, then, is the badge of courage of the Thirties, and the conception of self-realization concludes the novel and its surgical dissection of George's evolving personality. The little commitment of George to Catherine mirrors the larger commitment of Jerome, and the period of the Thirties as well, to mankind itself and to values of life and reality.

HUGH MACLENNAN AND THE CANADIAN MYTH

DOROTHY FARMILOE

Over the years, through a steadily deepening analysis of the national scene, Hugh MacLennan has been exploring the meaning of Canadianism; each of his novels, in some manner, has been a variation on this theme. His long study of all aspects of the Canadian character has peculiarly fitted him for the writing of *The Watch that Ends the Night*[1] in which he traces Canada's coming-of-age. More important, in this novel he has gone back to examine what he feels are the character-shaping protoforms of the Canadian identity as exemplified by the fur trader. In one magnificent chapter of *The Watch that Ends the Night* in which the boy Jerome escapes down the wilderness river in his canoe, Hugh MacLennan is giving us his version not only of the Canadian character, but of the Canadian myth.

The most rewarding, and probably the shortest, route into MacLennan's latest novels is through his essay "The People Behind this Peculiar Nation." In this brief study MacLennan wrote that the fur trade has been as basic to the Canadian character as the sea has been to England's; that nations as well as children tend to forget the events of early years; that these events sink into and become part of the national subconscious. The true makers of Canada, he maintains, were not the Victorians whose ghastly statues surround the Parliament Buildings in Ottawa, but the voyageurs:

> They were desperate men, and the story of their fabulous
> river voyages has no counterpart south of the border. It has
> no counterpart anywhere in the world, and if anyone wants
> to know why Canada is subtly different in character from
> the United States, it is to those men and to this period that
> he should look. (*Northern Lights*, p. 514).

"Hugh MacLennan and the Canadian Myth," by Dorothy Farmiloe. In *Mosaic*, 2-3 (Spring, 1969), pp. 1-9. By permission of *Mosaic*.

If we accept true myth as originating in either the historical or the religious background of a people and belonging to their collective subconscious, then it becomes clear that Hugh MacLennan is leading us, in this essay, toward his definition of the Canadian myth. In the significant section dealing with Jerome's childhood in *The Watch that Ends the Night,* pp. 173-219), MacLennan has consciously embodied in narrative form all the mythic elements of our early history that he had outlined in his essay.

This chapter is a flashback episode, one of many, in the life of Jerome Martell told partly in his words and partly in the words of the protagonist George Stewart. The boy's experience is a mythologized version of the early years of this country. Jerome, having inadvertently witnessed his mother's murder, flees the community of the lumber camp to face the utter loneliness of the virgin wilderness. The social myth pursues him in the form of the Engineer; here is Jerome's description of him:

> "There was a man that winter," he said, "that used to frighten me the way a snake frightens me now. There was nothing snake-like about his appearance, but there was a look in his eye, the way he had of looking at everybody. He never talked at all, and when he drank he drank sullenly. We all called him the Engineer because . . . he was the only man in camp who could keep the motorboat in repair. He was dark and lean and he had this queer, drawn look in his face, and he used to carry a spanner wherever he went. . . ." (*The Watch that Ends the Night*, p. 178).

The entire chapter is related with deliberate simplicity and understated emotion in passages that, like the one above suggesting the sullen ugliness of a mechanical civilization, are cumulatively and powerfully effective. In contrast to the Engineer, Jerome symbolizes the Voyageur. His lonely struggle to escape, his attitude to his predicament, his native fortitude and resourcefulness, all add up to a display of the same survival tactics that enabled the early coureurs de bois to exist in the wilderness. Jerome has enough presence of mind to take provisions for his flight in the form of sausage (the pemmican of the fur traders); he makes use of the natural protection of the forest in covering himself with pine needles; he escapes in his canoe (the voyageur's only means of transportation), the Engineer (society) following him in the motorboat. To continue categorizing in this manner, however, is to risk turning a very fine tale into a one-for-one allegory when it suggests so much more.

Jerome's name, for example. The obvious implication is that the name is French, suggesting something of French Canadian heritage—in this case, the river lore. But there is more to it than that. Jerome knows nothing of his real father; after his escape from the Engineer he makes his way to a railway station where he is discovered and adopted by a Protestant clergyman and his wife. Although his foster father is English, the name Martell, as Jerome finds out later, is of Huguenot origin, implying, in a Canadian adaptation, ambiguities of French Catholicism and English Protestantism. Both his first and last names have this significance. "Jerome," his foster father speculates, "generally only Roman Catholics are called Jerome." Thus MacLennan has cleverly and economically incorporated the four important ingredients of our native make-up into the personification of Jerome Martell—French, English, Protestant, Roman Catholic—for a genuinely Canadian symbolic figure. When Jerome says at one point that he does not know who he is, he exemplifies not only the search for the Canadian identity but the split personality caused by the two cultures in our national consciousness. This goes a long way towards explaining the paradox of his character as George sees it in the novel: "He was so boyish and yet he was so competent, he was so rugged and yet so vulnerable, so intelligent in some things and yet so naive in others" (p. 163).

Jerome is a re-creation of the early rivermen embodying the rugged nature of the French and Highland explorers—the men, as Mac-Lennan emphasizes in his essay, "who are behind Canada, and the attitude with which they faced their destiny is buried deep in the Canadian subconscious" (*Northern Lights*, p. 518). Martell means hammer, and we feel the hammer-like forcefulness of the adult Jerome's approach both in his direct method of wooing Catherine and in the episode concerning Shatwell's mistress where he forges his way into the hospital to operate on another doctor's patient without waiting for authorization. All the characteristics Jerome displays as *The Watch* unfolds are the inherent traits of bravery, stubbornness, pride—and "loneliness past modern comprehension" (*Northern Lights*, p. 516)—that were exhibited in the lives of the voyageurs.

There is also a suggestion of restrained strength in the significant river section where the writing flows with the fluid ease and hidden power of a great northern river. In the wonderful paragraph after Jerome knows he is safe from the Engineer, the river and the forest come to life for him; but more important than the stylistic felicity is that the boy and the canoe are an organic part of the environment:

> Now Jerome became aware of life all around him as birds called in the forest on either side of the river, he saw the white trunks of a stand of birch, and as the current at this point swerved in toward the shore, the carolling ring of bird calls was loud and near. . . . Jerome heard a snick and saw the flash of a trout's belly. He paddled on through clear water . . . and within ten minutes there were snicking flashes all around him as trout broke the surface to feed on early flies, the first run of the season in from the sea, quick, slim fish with bellies as bright as silver coins, firm and fierce from a winter of cold salt water as they drove up against the current to the beds where they had been spawned. . . . Still the tiny canoe throbbed down the stream, the boy in the stern. . . . (*The Watch*, p. 191).

The setting for this chapter is the primitive atmosphere of the wilderness unchanged from the early days before the comforts of civilization intruded. In those days it was "pork and beans, scouse and salted horse and lime juice against the scurvy, it was boils and the savagery of melancholy temper which comes when men live and eat like that" (*The Watch*, p. 174). Beginning with the violence of the mother's murder (violence is a favourite device of MacLennan's to initiate change) the adventure on the river becomes the traumatic experience—something of which always remains in the subconscious—that shapes the nation as well as the child. Again, in Jerome's words: "I just thought about the canoe and the river and I was so alert that everything I saw and did—everything—I still remember" (*The Watch*, p. 187).

Jerome's trip in the canoe is a Canadian counterpoint to Huck Finn's flight down the Mississippi on the raft and ought to occupy the same place in Canadian literature that Huck's holds in American. The tradition that has grown up around Mark Twain's tale involves the American myth of the hero who escapes from the dehumanizing restrictions of society to the freedom of the frontier.[2] Both Huck and Jerome are fleeing from a civilization they consider vicious; Huck from the murderous small towns of the Mississippi, Jerome from the murderous lumber camp. Huck's way of life is that of the outcast; so too is Jerome's. In the struggle for survival both boys transcend the world they leave to achieve mythic significance. While Mark Twain was largely unaware of what he had put into his novel, Hugh MacLennan has consciously included in his the elements inherent in our early development.[3] Jerome Martell's story is a re-enactment springing out of the symbols peculiar to Canadian history —the canoe, the river, the immense wilderness—embodied in a powerful and exciting narrative that emerges as a pure Canadian classic.

Canada's history is subtly different from that of any other country, as MacLennan emphasized in his essay. A unique Canadian myth must recognize the place the rivers and the wilderness which surrounded the early settlements have played in our development; Northrop Frye wonders if any other national consciousness has had so large an amount of the unknown, the unrealized, the humanly undigested, built into it.[4] Huck Finn's Mississippi is lined with small towns, and he has Jim for companionship. But Jerome is completely alone: "There were no lights on the shore, no cabins or houses, there was nothing but the forest, the sky, the moon, the river, the canoe and the logs floating down to the sea" (*The Watch*, p. 188). All that T. S. Eliot says in the familiar quotation from his essay is even more applicable to Jerome:

> Huck Finn is alone: there is no more solitary character in fiction. The fact that he has a father only emphasizes his loneliness; and he views his father with a terrifying detachment. So we come to see Huck himself in the end as one of

the permanent symbolic figures of fiction; not unworthy to take a place with Ulysses, Faust, Don Quixote, Don Juan, Hamlet and other great discoveries that man has made about himself. (*Adventures of Huckleberry Finn*, p. 322).[5]

As in *Huckleberry Finn* it is the river that gives the important Part Five of *The Watch* its form and its mythic quality. It is as much a river-god as the Mississippi,[6] with a will and a mind of its own. It is a live thing. During his flight Jerome watched it "gurgling and sighing as it strained through the scrub and deadfalls . . . living water" (p. 186), and "often he passed floating logs and once he came up with a raft of them lodged on a hidden rock and damming the current, the water washing over and making the whole raft pitch and heave as though things were alive under it" (pp. 187-188). The river is both preserver and destroyer, sheltering Jerome in the lee of an island while his mother's murderer goes by, but ready in an instant to crush the tiny canoe in a log jam. It is the river that takes him back to civilization.

This is the qualifying difference between Huck and Jerome that points up the conscious artistry of MacLennan. At the end of Twain's book Huck "lights out for the territory ahead of the rest," which is a false, or at any rate a limited, resolution. Civilization eventually encroaches on whatever literal territory we attempt to escape to, and the American frontier was disappearing even as Mark Twain was writing. Hugh MacLennan is less idealistic in this respect than his American counterpart. He realizes that there are no easy answers, that there may be no answers at all, that the problems are not solved by running away. After his canoe trip Jerome rejoins society to wage a lonely battle for his own moral values, a battle that results in the rejection of his foster father's religion. And later, when he renounces Canadian isolationism in the Thirties to fight in the Spanish Civil War, he is still, like Huck, the lonely natural child that society never tames. But there is no Territory waiting for Jerome. George assesses the whole situation in terms of the novel's controlling symbol:

> The canoe in which he had issued from the forest had now taken him out into the ocean. A canoe in an ocean, at night, with a hurricane rising. Jerome, Myself, Everyone. (*The Watch*, p. 289).

Tom Sawyer and Huck Finn are a composite (of Twain himself, as Eliot suggests), the one socially acceptable, wanting domestic life of a conventional kind, seeking prosperity; the other indifferent to these things, an outcast, alienated from society. It is even more true that George Stewart and Jerome Martell are opposite sides of one coin; each exemplifies not only the respective qualities outlined by Eliot, but both of MacLennan's heroes are closely correlated by being married to the same woman in an Enoch Arden plot. Thus MacLennan further formulates the paradox of our national character. It is one of the ironic twists of the book that Jerome is married to the invalid Catherine who is, as his mistress Norah insists, "a symbol of our sick civilization." Norah says: "She's not well and Jerome is so strong" (p. 277).

The correlation between George and Jerome brings out a further dimension of the myth. Jerome remains for the most part a flashback character, symbolically more alive in the past than in the present. Yet George has some of Jerome's ability to act in moments of crisis; if he has lost the animal-like bravery of Jerome, he has maintained a fortitude and integrity of his own. He is, in fact, a latter-day Jerome whom civilization has tamed—the Canadian as MacLennan sees him today. George recognizes the affinity between Jerome and himself when both are waiting for the result of Catherine's operation:

> Then I became conscious of him coming very close to me even though he did not move. Suddenly he seemed to be inside me, *to be me*, and I became dizzy and weak. (p. 364. The italics are MacLennan's.)

In this electrifying epiphany in which the two men are finally and fully equated, MacLennan seems to be saying that the past is still alive in us, that the force of the myth is still operative.

The Watch that Ends the Night is the story of Canada's evolution told, appropriately enough, by George Stewart who is a radio commentator as well as a freelance writer of political articles. It is significant that George holds a degree in history; as the story opens he is lecturing part-time at the university. He is well-qualified, therefore, to comment on the past as well as the present, particularly the important Thirties and Forties that form the backdrop for much of the novel's setting:

> While the war thundered on, Canada unnoticed grew into a nation at last. This cautious country which had always done more than she had promised, had always endured in silence while others reaped the glory—now she became alive and to us within her excitingly so. My work brought me close to the heart of this changing land (p. 317).

It is easier to accept what MacLennan is doing with myth when we view Jerome's story through the eyes of a historian. George is a logical and acceptable spokesman for the author; he quietly relates events in the life of Jerome Martell that parallel the growth of Canada itself. Jerome spends his early years in the wilderness and his adolescence in the "semi-ghost town of a colonial past" (p. 195). Except for the river episode we are not told much of Jerome's life at this period. (MacLennan has explored the colonial-mentality phase of our national past at greater length elsewhere.) When Jerome accepts urban living—in his case, in Montreal—and final involvement on the world front, his destiny and Canada's have moved into the present. George, rejected by the army on two counts, remains to comment on the war in his radio broadcasts and on Jerome in his after-hours. Foreshortened into one man's lifetime the superb history parallels are there as an integral part of the pattern and fabric of the novel.

Hugh MacLennan's long study of the mystique of Canadianism has prepared him well for the task he set himself in *The Watch that Ends the Night.* Each of his novels expresses the Canadian character in one of its social aspects: *Barometer Rising* proclaims the leap from colonial mentality to a new Canadian identity; *Two Solitudes* probes the French-English conflict with considerable insight and sympathy, while *The Precipice* does the same for Canadian-American relations; *Each Man's Son* explores the vestiges of Calvinist influence. On the surface level *The Watch* examines the Depression years when people "caught politics just as a person catches religion" (p. 223). The latest work, *Return of the Sphinx*, picks up many of the earlier arguments and weaves them into a father-son relationship, a sequel to *Each Man's Son.* In this novel, as in most of the others, the social ideas tend to over-balance the imaginative handling of the material with the unfortunate result that the lesser characters become stereotypes. Bulstrode and Latendresse in *The Sphinx* are cardboard caricatures. Only *The Watch that Ends the Night*, in every way Mac-Lennan's best work, avoids this failing. Even the minor characters in *The Watch*—Norah and Harry, for example—are well-rounded.

Some of MacLennan's best writing is in his unforgettable descriptions of the Canadian climate and countryside. If there is a common denominator in his work, it is that of the land itself. This is what Alan Ainslie sees, after driving coast-to-coast, at the end of *Return of the Sphinx*:

> Images of the land: the long wash of the decisive ocean against the granite; sunlight spangling the mist over the estuary the old navigator had mistaken for the Northwest Passage leading to the indispensable dream; the prairie wind almost as visible above the wheat as ruffling through it; the antlers of a bull elk cascading down the side of a Rocky Mountain; arrows of wild geese shooting off into the twilight over the delta of the Athabasca. . . .
>
> He went to the window and saw lake and forest married in perfect silence.
>
> The vast land. Too vast even for fools to ruin all of it. . . .
>
> He believed it would endure. (pp. 302-303).

This, as description, is typical of MacLennan's style, but it performs other functions as well. MacLennan sees this vast land with its lakes and rivers as one of the basic elements in our unique myth, and the love for the land remains, conscious or unconscious, in us as part of our collective personality; the continuing popularity of the nature poets attests to our peculiar bond with the land. This atavistic affinity with nature is symbolized in MacLennan's novels by the summer cottage in the Laurentians. It is here that Jerome and Catherine are happiest; it is here that Alan Ainslie and his son return, though separately, for spiritual communion with their deepest roots. At the cottage Alan feels a warmness come back to his soul, and Daniel, after fishing in the canoe for his supper, cooks his fish in the coolness of the cottage and feels deeply satisfied with the goodness of everything. Out on the lake in front of the cottage Jerome tells George the story of his childhood which is incorporated into the river episode in Part Five of *The Watch that Ends the Night.*

This significant section of the novel is the finest piece of writing Hugh MacLennan has ever done and is the best attempt so far by any novelist to define the Canadian myth. One might question, perhaps, whether Canadians today identify with the voyageurs to the extent indicated by MacLennan, but one cannot question the existence of this particular myth taken within the context of his definition of the Canadian character. He has brilliantly proven his case in the characterization of Jerome Martell and George Stewart. In the process he has added a new dimension to his own writing and posed an incentive to further exploration on the part of other writers by opening up the subcontinent of Canadian myth.

NOTES

1. The works of Hugh MacLennan cited in this essay, in the order in which they occur, are as follows: *The Watch that Ends the Night* (Toronto, 1959); "The People Behind this Peculiar Nation," *Northern Lights*, ed. George E. Nelson (New York, 1960), 513-18; *Return of the Sphinx* (New York 1967).

2. For the symbolic significance of *Huckleberry Finn* see T.S. Eliot, "An Introduction to Huckleberry Finn," in *Adventures of Huckleberry Finn*, ed. Sculley Bradley, Richmond Croom Beatty, E. Hudson Long (New York, 1961), 320-27; also James M. Cox, "Remarks on the Sad Initiation of Huckleberry Finn," *Mark Twain's Huckleberry Finn*, ed. Barry Marks (Boston, 1959), 65-74.

3. This claim is adequately supported by MacLennan's own thesis in "The People Behind this Peculiar Nation." When we compare the novel and the essay—as I am doing in this paper—the conclusion that MacLennan has consciously used the elements of the fur trade as myth is inescapable.

4. *Literary History of Canada*, ed. Carl F. Klinck (Toronto, 1965), p. 826.

5. Reprinted by permission of Mrs. Valerie Eliot.

6. See Lionel Trilling, "The Greatness of Huckleberry Finn," *Adventures of Huckleberry Finn* (above, note 2), 310-20.

RETURN OF THE SPHINX

J. M. STEDMOND

Hugh MacLennan's revisit to the theme of "two solitudes" in *Return of the Sphinx* . . . seems prompted almost by a sense of duty rather than the spur of new insights. His attention as novelist is as much on the gap between generations as on Quebec's quiet revolution. Discussions of Canada's political and cultural problems occur in rather wooden interchanges among the characters, but these are almost incidental to the story of disparate love matches between youth and maturity. Contentions, such as that French Canadian separatism is a substitute for lost Catholicism, that the problem is not economic but psychological, and that all revolutions have neurotic roots, are presumably illustrated by making the principal revolutionary, Aimé Latendresse, a spoiled priest and suggesting that his cat's-paw, Daniel Ainslie, suffers from a mother complex. But the characters tend to become spokesmen for points of view, and thus to an extent rhetorical devices rather than imaginative creations.

The leading figure in the story is Alan Ainslie, rather awkwardly borrowed from an earlier novel, *Each Man's Son*, at the end of which he was a child orphaned by the violent deaths of his parents. There is not much carry-over into the later novel. Ainslie is now a widower with a grown-up son and daughter and has just entered parliament as the minister of a newly created Department of Cultural Affairs. His wife (recently killed in a cruelly meaningless accident) was French Canadian, so his son and daughter represent a fusion of the two races, and the turbulence within them is like that within the nation. Each of the two seeks love with an older partner, who also happens to be a French expatriate. Some of the symbolism is obtrusive, and the mythic overtones raised by the title, the suggestions that Canada's drift towards chaos is in some way typical of a general world situation, though intriguing, are not finally convincing.

"From "Letters in Canada: Fiction," by J.M. Stedmond. In *University of Toronto Quarterly*, 37 (July, 1968), pp. 383-84. By permission of University of Toronto Press.

The impact is dulled by the Galsworthian aura surrounding characters with names like Gabriel Fleury and Chantal Ainslie. The echoes of *Middlemarch* roused by calling a strangely concocted politician Bulstrode are oddly out of place in a contemporary Montreal-Ottawa setting.

BEAUTY AND THE BEAST

Douglas Spettigue

Return of the Sphinx is not only an unexpected sequel to *Each Man's Son*, it sounds at times as though it were meant to round off the whole MacLennan canon. The son of *Each Man's Son* was Alan MacNeil whose father, Archie, escaped the Cape Breton mines as a prizefighter only to be exploited and ruined in the States. At the end he reached home, killed his wife and her lover and died before his son's eyes, a sequence recalled in *Return of the Sphinx*. In the interim the brilliant but guilt-ridden Dr. Ainslie has raised and educated Alan as his own son. In the new novel that same Alan, now Alan Ainslie, is Minister of Culture in an over-aged government faced with the long-expected Quebec revolt. His half-French son, Daniel, is an active if naive separatist whose involvement costs Alan his career, while his lovely and emancipated daughter, Chantal, offers herself as mistress to Alan's old friend Gabriel Fleury.

That's all. The rest is reminiscence, reflection and long topical dialogues. If *Each Man's Son* showed Alan's escape into security, education and service from an insecure, a primitive and a futureless past this novel shows the revolt, by his children, against all he has accomplished and believed in. This is a sequel and a completion in many ways.

Since it is now some years since George Woodcock first identified Hugh MacLennan's Odyssean heroes, it is time to note a regression or at least a change in their quests. Neil Macrae, the protagonist of MacLennan's first (published) novel, came home from the First World War to a waiting Penelope. He came like Ulysses in disguise, because he came to a society that had closed its gates against his youth. But the Halifax explosion, product of the war and symbolic of its effects, swept the old order to oblivion and freed the creative energies of the Neils and Pennys for the building of a new and better society. *Two*

"Beauty and the Beast" [Review Article], by Douglas Spettigue, in *Queen's Quarterly*, 74 (1967), pp. 762-65. By permission of the author.

Solitudes examined the effects of a Second World War on a bi-cultural Canada still dominated by the old commercial English families on the one hand and a paternal Church on the other. Ulysses this time is a young French Canadian writer who fights free of his society in order to be its interpreter in fiction to a world that knows it not. The same is true of Bruce West of *The Precipice*, but here the antagonist is American materialism and the misdirected energy is not released in war but in the guilt-driven rush toward national suicide. Both Paul Tallard and Bruce West see their function as explaining Canada to herself and to the world, while Lucy Lassiter of *The Precipice* returns to her erring American husband to leaven the hysterical American lump with a little Presbyterian-Canadian restraint. The Canada of the first novel was the one the twentieth century might belong to; the Canada of the next two was one whose self-knowledge, borne of her peculiar internal tensions, would make her the honest broker of the postwar world.

The familiar weakness of these earlier novels was the preponderance of thesis; the characters were too busy being spokesmen ever to become people. There was a one-for-one correspondence of character and idea. Only the first part of *Two Solitudes* showed the MacLennan strength in dealing with elemental characters in close association with the land. That strength revealed itself in *Each Man's Son* where a new concentration and depth were achieved through dividing Ulysses into three, as it were—a physical, an emotional and an intellectual protagonist. It was the success of the first of these, Archie McNeil, that led Warren Tallman to the thesis that MacLennan's real commitment was not, as the author himself supposed, to the classical world Dr. Ainslie admires but to the primitive and crude.

A link among many early MacLennan characters was the voyage to the eastern Mediterranean that was both a specific Odyssey and an attempt to draw on the beauty and order of classical culture to humanize North America. The triumph of Dr. Ainslie, who translated Homer religiously before breakfast, over Archie MacNeil presumably showed the power of Beauty over the Beast. The unrecorded education of the orphan Alan by Ainslie, like the later adoption of Jerome by the Martells, was an attempt at maintaining North American energy while civilizing it.

The Watch that Ends the Night combined the civilized and the crude in the "primitive" super-doctor Jerome Martell, who waged a lone battle against fascism on behalf of the adopted culture it threatened. That novel also extended the range of Hugh MacLennan's probing of the bases of the Canadian and of the modern psyche. To account for the threat to civilization, it showed war, depression and the Bomb hastening the collapse of traditional values and of the social and political structures based on them. But in the end there is no questing youth left to go forth as creative artist. Catherine's explosions of beauty were private, and Catherine is dead. Only the middle-aged George Stewart is left, learning to live with himself in personal and religious terms in a society that can no longer believe in itself.

"The "explosion" image from *Barometer Rising* went inward in the subsequent novels. The Preface to *Each Man's Son* introduced a "beast behind the unlocked door" that was the Calvinistic God. That beast was in fact the potential for violence that Jerome says "is in us" all and bursts out wherever it has been damned. Similarly, the sea of the early quests became the sea of the subconscious in *The Watch that Ends the Night* as well as the fate that overwhelms us all, while the quester's ship became a personal canoe in that rising ocean. Here, too, the quest gained universality as each character became a Ulysses or a Telemachus seeking the father or being sought. In the modern world Everyman is lost and what he must find is his own reconciliation with life and death, a substitute for what once was a sustaining faith.

With *Return of the Sphinx* the heroic quest is over. Two fathers lose their sons, a boy is drawn to a mother-mistress, a girl finds a father-lover and Alan relives the loss of his constant Penelope. These are the foreground actions for which the background is an intense battle of ideas on the themes of unity and separation. In the end the ideas—all ideas—are shown to be unreal. Reality is in the brief touching of bodies, in rare moments of peace beside a northern lake, in being young and believing and then in growing old and learning the futility of everything except perhaps sympathy and the old cycle of life itself. Love of the land breathes through this book, love of *la nation* whether the greater or the lesser; but *Return of the Sphinx* strips us of our illusions about the importance or even the necessary survival of Canada. It says some very forthright things about America and the modern world. It lays on the line much that has only been implicit before. But even while it reaches for more and more complications in its political dialogues, it reduces the human quest to a new simplicity: all fanaticism is a spilling over of energy that ought to have spilled into love: the world has had its creative moments but ours is a destructive one; the little role that our country might have played in the supreme task of building a higher civilization—that white city on a hill that Jerome Martell had dreamed of—now is seen abandoned; democracy, education, the rooted family all are seen now as a wistful dream, panaceas that no intelligent modern can believe in. Ours is the era when all nationalisms must be sacrificed to the superpowers and all cultures collapse before their automated materialism. Things fall apart, as Yeats says; sheer anarchy is loosed upon the world.

It is the "rough beast" of Yeats' "The Second Coming" that returns in this novel. The human dream of order might, in this age of wonders, have had its fruition. Instead, man's energies have turned the other way, toward breaking down what took so long to build up. "One more step would have freed us all, but the sphinx returned." For the Hugh MacLennan who once aimed to bring "a little graciousness" back into our lives, this is a bitter pill to swallow. For the author whose nationalism has been a byword, the acknowledgement of the powers of the American beast without and the separatist beast within must be painful indeed.

Of course a wise hopelessness is one of the modern poses. The last two novels acknowledge the loss of religious faith that Hugh MacLennan seems to regard as a mortal wound. It is a stubborn piety on Ainslie's part that still can hope that "God has some plan for us." But life goes on. A little warmth creeps around at the end as Alan attends a rural wedding. There are moments of love. There is a Dostoevskian faith in the power of the meek to endure. And there is a touching belief in the northern land, "too vast even for fools to ruin all of it."

There is a lot of talk in this book, more perhaps than a novel

should hold, especially a novel that exposes the futility of talk—
but this is just the point. Against all that talk the few foreground
actions loom large as dramatic scenes: the love of Gabriel and
Chantal, Alan's and Daniel's visits to the cottage, Daniel's mad ride,
the interview with Bulstrode. Continuity and completeness have
been replaced by moments or memories of tenderness or of horror
as the constructive or the destructive forces dictate. This apparently
is all we can look for, at least until a creative cycle is renewed. "The
Sphinx has returned to the world before, after all."

WINTER AND THE NIGHT-PEOPLE

WILLIAM H. NEW

The first sixty pages of *Return of the Sphinx* are among the worst that Hugh MacLennan has written. A blunt statement: but a book like this one, which contends even in fiction with the thorniest political problem in Canada today, is bound to arouse blunt statements. It is not paradoxical, I hope, to add that this is in many ways MacLennan's most important novel too, which makes the faults in it seem larger than under other circumstances they would. The novel emerges not only out of his earlier works and relates to them by both theme and imagery; it also demonstrates a distinct advancement. What before had been nebulous and sometimes even noncommittal in the resolution to his works has here been extended into a tragic vision—for Canada, for the characters, and for the world.

Ambitious? Yes. Worthwhile? Indeed, yes. But successful only on occasion. Briefly, the novel concerns the conflict that assails Alan Ainslie, federal Minister of Culture in a cabinet that seems to have both Diefenbaker and Pearson figures in it (a situation ripe with fictional promise in its own right, but by the way). His French Canadian wife has been killed by a truck overturning in a freak accident; his daughter, Chantal, is in love with his best friend, an emigrant Frenchman near his own age named Gabriel Fleury; and his son, Daniel, tortured by a Jansenist schooling and by awakening sexual urges, torn between respect for his gentle father and antagonism towards all things and all people not French Canadian and of another generation, is becoming more and more involved in the Separatist cause. For Alan the problem is only partly a political one; much more so is it emotional—at a national level, where his commitment to the cause of Confederation is both deep and honest, and at a personal level, where his memory of past happiness with his

"Winter and the Night-People," by William H. New. In *Canadian Literature*, No. 36 (Spring, 1968), pp. 26-33. Published in *Articulating West* by W.H. New (Toronto: New Press, 1972). Reprinted by permission of the author and the publisher.

wife is so strong that he has really lost contact with the world that is growing up, here and now, around him. The two are obviously symbolically related. Alan's tragedy is that he does not recognize what is happening until it is too late, until events have taken place that divide him irrecovably from his position in government and effectively from his children. His world, at the end of the novel, is different from the one he has seen at the beginning, although in the background there still broods a hint of the ideal world which Alan has been conscious of and which MacLennan himself has been concerned with throughout all of his fiction.

We have met these characters before in MacLennan's work. Chantal, idealistic, young and therefore confident, at once sophisticated and naive, intelligent, capable, and determined, has under different guise appeared as Penny Wain in *Barometer Rising* and Sally Martell in *The Watch that Ends the Night*. She performs much the same function here—the representative of the realization of young love—but she is less of a stick figure than the other two and so more satisfactory as a character. Daniel has developed out of Marius Tallard, the young rebel and Oedipally-motivated father-hater in *Two Solitudes*, but again he is more rounded and more credible. Whereas Marius had been shallowly drawn, a shadow figure defeated as much by his own character as by the System he was reacting against, Daniel is by contrast brimful with talent and possibilities. Tragic again is his commitment to an increasingly narrowing cause, for the mistakes he makes in judgment cease to be the excusable sins of youth when they affect the life of the nation itself.

Alan Ainslie is, of course, quite literally the boy Alan (MacNeil) Ainslie from *Each Man's Son*, now grown-up—trying, as so many MacLennan characters do, to forget his origins (wandering father, murdered mother), and attempting by this means to attach himself and his family to a kind of order it has never really been his to know. We have seen this in Neil Macrae in *Barometer Rising*, in Jerome Martell, and even to some extent in Paul Tallard. In all the earlier books MacLennan has implied that the order is achievable, that the characters have conquered the major obstacles in the way of their happiness. But in fact there is always another note present as well, which, in imagery involving winter and darkness, hints of isolation and of further conflict yet to come. Neil and Penny, for example, are reunited by the end of *Barometer Rising,* and the Canadian nation they represent has severed itself successfully from the nineteenth-century control of Great Britain. But the language is not altogether joyful: "They paused on the narrow, snowbanked platform and watched the lights of the coaches disappear around the next curve and heard the dying echoes of the whistle reverberating through the forest." Similarly, *Two Solitudes* ends with Paul Tallard and Heather Methuen together, with autumn golden, and yet things are not really stable: "Only in the far north on the tundra was the usual process of life abruptly fractured"; the nation is going into war, "knowing against her will that she was not unique but like all the others, alone with history, with science, with the future." *Each Man's Son,* moreover, ends with Ainslie adopting Alan MacNeil—which closes a novel largely about ignorance and single-mindedness, but also intimates the beginning of another phase of human conflict; Ainslie "has no sense of the distance he had walked or what time of night it was. He stood in the darkness outside his own house for a long while, hearing the sound of the broken water in the brook." And *The Watch that Ends the Night,* which closes at the end of a summer with George Stewart discovering a kind of metaphysical peace, ends also with his knowing the world about him as a shadow, knowing politics as an unreal thing in that world, and knowing light only insofar as his life is now illuminated from within himself. *Return of the Sphinx* picks up these darker threads of MacLennan's thought, in a study of the breakup of the order of a single man's family and a parallel disruption of society at large. No answers exist—only the sphinx—and this novel, too, closes with "the long snows" approaching.

* * *

The extension of character into political affairs, by a kind of modified allegory, is also a feature of all of MacLennan's books—most demonstrably forced in *Two Solitudes* and *The Precipice,* where the one-to-one correspondence between character and political entity is so defined as to make any proffered solutions seem facile. The allegory is most competently handled where it seems effortless, where the technique becomes an integral part of the message.

Barometer Rising, for example, is brilliantly structured, yet the reader is conscious less of the form than of the reality of the novel's focal situation; and *The Watch that Ends the Night* succeeds because the political allegory is implicit in the imagery rather than explicitly enunciated by the central characters. *Return of the Sphinx* wavers a little between these two groups, but ultimately, because of its overt commitment, it most closely approximates *The Precipice*, except that large parts of it are better written.

MacLennan uses here some of the same image patterns he has used before, and handles them well. Night, winter, flowers are all important strands in exploring the conflict. The story takes place in Eastern Canada as a hot, humid summer is settling down on Montreal. It is the ripe time for riots in North America. The oppressive climate and oppressive situations (real or imagined) seem to come together then and, if causes exist in the mind of a people, they can manifest themselves in forceful, concerted mass, and therefore often dangerous and violent ways. Some emotionally sensitive individuals, like Daniel Ainslie, will be used by the power structure that orders any political demonstration, and if this turns to riot, they are consumed. Others, like Alan, will be so committed to another ideal that they may be overwhelmed by the moment. Still others, like Gabriel Fleury, are taken out of their personal isolation during a time like this; if they discover the real meaning of love, they survive. This last situation is figured early in the novel when we are told that Gabriel "was not a good golfer—he preferred winter to summer on account of the skiing, at which he was very good—but it was the only summer game he knew and physical exercise was the one permanent security in his life." The problem is the same one presented to George Stewart in *The Watch that Ends the Night*. He has to discover that the winter snows—symbolic of an innocence that this country perhaps once knew—are no longer the only identity to be met with. He has to learn the games of summer, in effect, so that in any season he can survive, but in doing so he will learn the facts of heat and discord as well. So with Alan, whose happiness (Constance, the children, a lake and cottage and a summer when "the daisies were like snow in the high Gaspesian meadows") lies in the past; and so with Daniel as well (whose blinding focus on the present is jolted when he discovers not only the identity of his Cape Breton grandfather—the Nova Scotia/French combination in the place name a probably unintentional added irony here—but also how alike they are).

This tension between past and present is given further development in the overtly political passages in the book, but first we must see that Gabriel's character is extended by the imagery of night and flowers. His name, for one thing, and his recurrent association with nicotianas ("they're night flowers and I'm only here at night") are a constant reminder of the possibility of flourishing and of being at peace with one's environment. His union with the younger generation, in his love for Chantal Ainslie, is a happy one for them both, and the last innocence is gone, the flowers "of late summer were in bud." For Daniel and Alan the contact between generations is more difficult, and when the book ends with winter coming on and with Alan outside the city contemplating the landscape, thinking, "The vast land—too vast even for fools to ruin all of it," we can see that symbolically the ideals of Confederation, cooperation and stability, are still held as possibilities within man's reach. But for Alan it seems more like an insistent belief in the mask than an acceptance of the night and the heat that influence the human landscape.

Daniel, like Chantal, also has the opportunity to respond to both the city and the land, and as his first sexual encounter is with a woman from the older generation, the parallel with his sister is strengthened. Chantal is learning from Gabriel as well as giving to him, however. Daniel is affected rather less by Marielle's wisdom than she is carried away by his impulsive desire for satisfaction and revenge. The "revenge" is against many things—his Jesuit schooling, his conscience, his father, his mother's death, *les Anglais*, the American influence in his society and among young people, and so on. MacLennan's extension of the image patterns into the political sphere becomes obvious in Daniel's reaction to his city:

> It's fantastic, the truth you can see in this city at night. You can go for miles without seeing a single *Anglais.* They know no more about this city than the English knew about India. When I learn more about television techniques I want a program about this city after dark. About *la nation* after dark.

The camera spying. The camera working as if it had a mind
of its own. The camera just telling me what to do with it.
The people speaking in broken sentences. That's where the
truth is, in broken sentences. Their expressions when you
catch them with the truth on their faces. The people are
smoldering. There's not enough room for them any more.
They live in the city like a huge African kraal with the forests all around them. The lights on the snow in the streets,
the dirty snow in the streets. . . .

In the city, in Montreal, the mask of innocence that the land has
held before itself no longer exists, but it is not a world of sophisti-
cation which by and large has replaced it. Gabriel Fleury is sophisticated, is part of the night, and he survives; but in the world Daniel
recognizes only negation exists: surrender to material pleasure, decadence, bombing (ironically for the sake of a culture), and rioting
simply for the sake of being divisive. Even this is a way of living to
which he wants to attach himself, but he cannot. For all his activities,
he remains the spectator-television interviewer, trying to escape himself and discovering only another kind of incarceration.

The political problem of *Canadien* separatism is of course a
particularly grave one in Canada at this time. MacLennan is right to
feel that this can be the focus of a work of fiction, but when he
writes a work of this kind he is creating something that seems less
readily apprehensible by the Canadian imagination than by the
American or English one. All those works in Canadian literature
that apparently emphasize sociological phenomena, for example—
The Loved and the Lost, *The Master of the Mill*, *Scratch One
Dreamer*, *The Man from Glengarry*—are all much more obviously
studies in the psychology of an individual conscience. Such a cate-
gorization is less obvious, I think, in works by C. P. Snow or Robert
Penn Warren, and the disposition of American writers towards
political criticism is what perhaps lies behind Edmund Wilson's
approval of both MacLennan's *The Precipice* and the novels of
Morley Callaghan. In these works something of man-the-Canadian-
political-animal comes closest to the surface. But *Return of the
Sphinx*, political as it is, captures only some of the character of
either the country or the separatist question.

* * *

Canadians seem, in other words, to be much more addicted to the onlooker-interviewer role than most are willing to admit. Daniel and Alan Ainslie are our men, that is, just as George Stewart was in *The Watch that Ends the Night*—no matter how stuffy, thwarted, or unaware any of them might appear. MacLennan is right to set up this kind of character, right to interpret much about the nation this way, and curiously wrong when for some reason he locates a different kind of character in the West. He suggests that Westerners are delighted with Quebec's threatened withdrawal from the nation, for that event would give them a wealthy independence themselves, and he is wrong. Westerners, plain and simply, are the onlookers again, goaded in this decade into calling a plague on both houses, which they locate specifically in Toronto and Montreal, whose perennial opposition is now more than just high school rivalry. It is a continuation of a historic clash of cultures, which MacLennan himself implies in his book, but never makes clear, and it is this local antagonism, misunderstood by both locales, who both erroneously consider themselves representative of half the nation, that has been grotesquely magnified into an almost insoluble problem.

Like Daniel and Alan Ainslie, each side is magnificently sure of the other side's position. In this lies inevitable tragedy, for it demonstrates a previous foreclosure on both imagination and understanding. When Daniel thinks: "Endlessly the French Canadians talked of their deprived past and what did that do except weaken their purpose to make the future theirs?", both he and MacLennan have seized on a major truth underlying the whole situation. The parallel United Empire Loyalist-Upper Canada syndrome that afflicts some English Canadians, valuing some invalid sense of historic superiority, also prevents some people from preparing adequately for the future. Together these underline the fact that not only is the conflict in the present emerging out of the past, it is also very much of the past, still based on attitudes that most of the nation's people—from whatever cultural source (many young Westerners, for example, do not regard themselves as being *English* Canadian particularly)—do not here and now share. Daniel's immaturity is shown in that he does not trust his perception of truth; instead, he goes along with the riots and the bombs, which solve nothing. Alan's generation is by and large no better, for its members, violent in their own way, talk and talk, and again solve nothing.

It is interesting, at this point, to place the political argument of this book beside that in Peter Weiss's absurdist and terrifying play *Marat/Sade*. Part of the dialogue is apropos:

> Sade: Nature herself would watch unmoved / if we destroy-
> ed the entire human race / I hate Nature / this pas-
> sionless spectator this unbreakable ice-berg-face / that
> can bear everything / this goads us to greater and
> greater acts / Haven't we always beaten down those
> weaker than ourselves / . . . . /
>
> Marat: What you call the indifference of Nature / is your
> own lack of compassion / . . . . /
>
> Sade: No small emotions please / Your feelings were never
> petty / For you just as for me / only the most ex-
> treme actions matter /
>
> Marat: If I am extreme I am not extreme in the same way as
> you / Against Nature's silence I use action / In the
> vast indifference I invent a meaning / I don't watch
> unmoved I intervene / and say that this and this are
> wrong / and I work to alter them and improve them /
> The important thing / is to pull yourself up by your
> own hair / to turn yourself inside out / and see the
> whole world with fresh eyes . . . . (I, 12).

One of the many fascinating things about this play is that its technique of depicting plays within plays forces us all into roles both as spectators and actors: all implicated in whatever guilts, animal motives, insanities and oppressions may be represented. To-wards the end, Roux, the fettered radical, is still shouting out "When will you learn to see / When will you learn to take sides" as pande-monium engulfs him. What we do see above all else is the extent to which both Marat and Sade intellectualize humanity, and there-fore, though opposites, how much they are alike. The other oppo-sites—freedom / confinement; sanity / madness—also come in a sense to be indistinguishable, for one cannot identify which is which. But we are actors as well as spectators in such a play, and so if we respond at all these are truths for our own lives as well.

MacLennan's novel bears, it seems to me, enough likeness to Weiss's theme to make this digression reasonable. In Alan and Daniel, and in the views of Canada which they represent, we have just such intellectualizations coming into conflict. In the demonstrations Daniel plans, and the resultant riots which destroy Alan as a political figure, are just such unidentifiable motives as those of the revolution and the madmen of Charenton. Liberty? But the Québecois have liberties under federal law now that would be lost to them if they seceded. Equality? Fraternity? Yet as both Hugh MacLennan and Peter Weiss show, these desires are not necessarily distinguishable from the desire to exercise power.

The difference between the two writers is partly in technique, partly in the fact that Weiss does not draw a moral; his effect lies in his presentation and in the extent to which that alone can cause us to pull ourselves up by our own hair and see the world with fresh eyes. MacLennan, on the other hand, guides the reader to a point of view rather more deliberately, and the sadness of this is that the novel would have been more powerful had the characters and the images been capable of doing it on their own. For all the novel's political importance and for all the clarity with which the author views some political situations, no novel can absolutely succeed unless the characters come to life. With *Return of the Sphinx* we are up against a problem that has plagued MacLennan throughout his work: much of the dialogue is stilted, therefore lifeless, and the characters, who in other situations can be perfectly credible, will occasionally die. Regrettably, at those times, the novel dies with them. MacLennan can write magnificent monologues; of this there is no question, but so much of the dialogue is simply punctuated monologue that it becomes incredible. Where it is good, the formal language is inherently part of the situation being presented. Some of the arguments between Alan and Daniel, for example, and the passages of House of Commons debate are handled well. But where the conversations should be informal, even if they are not exactly relaxed, the language remains repetitive and starched:

> "He's wasting his life."
> "Can you be so sure he is?"
> "Oh yes, I can be sure."

This sort of thing is so constructed as to be artificial, too formalized to seem natural, and it occurs so often that one's attention shifts from the heart of the book to its method. It is a frustrating novel because it promises so much, and wavers so much too. For Mac-Lennan scholars it will be a key work, one which shows not only his descriptive abilities but also his consciousness of the tragic possibilities in modern life. For many more readers its topic will make it an interesting enough narrative to warrant reading. But for very few, unfortunately, in spite of its potential, will it be the impetus for seeing the world with eyes that have been made fresh.

BIBLIOGRAPHY

A. NOVELS BY MACLENNAN

Barometer Rising (New York: Duell, Sloan and Pearce, 1941). Paperback ed., Introd. Hugo McPherson, New Canadian Library, 8 (Toronto: McClelland and Stewart, 1958).

Two Solitudes (Toronto: Collins, 1945). Paperback ed. Laurentian Library, 1 (Toronto: Macmillan, 1967).

The Precipice (Toronto: Collins, 1948). Paperback ed. Popular Library (New York, n.d.).

Each Man's Son (Toronto: Macmillan, 1951). Paperback ed., Introd. A. Lucas, New Canadian Library, 30 (Toronto: McClelland and Stewart, 1965).

The Watch that Ends the Night (New York: Charles Scribner's Sons, 1959). Paperback ed. Signet Books (New American Library of Canada, 1961).

Return of the Sphinx (New York: Charles Scribner's Sons, 1967).

B. OTHER BOOKS BY MACLENNAN

Oxyrhynchus, an Economic and Social Study (Princeton: Princeton U.P., 1935; reprtd. Amsterdam: Hackert, 1968).

Canadian Unity and Quebec, together with Emile Vaillancourt, J.P. Humphrey (Montreal, 1942), 16 pp.

Cross-Country (Toronto: Collins, 1949).

Thirty and Three, ed. Dorothy Duncan (Toronto: Macmillan, 1954).

Scotchman's Return and Other Essays (Toronto: Macmillan, 1960).

Ed. *McGill, the Story of a University* (London: George Allen & Unwin, 1960).

Seven Rivers of Canada (Toronto: Macmillan, 1961).

The Colour of Canada (Toronto: McClelland and Stewart, 1967).

C. UNCOLLECTED ARTICLES BY MACLENNAN ON LITERATURE, HISTORY, AND CANADIAN PROBLEMS (SELECTED)

"Roman History and Today," *Dalhousie Review*, 15 (1936), pp. 67-78.

"Culture, Canadian Style," *Saturday Review of Literature*, 25 (March 28, 1942), pp. 3-4, 18-20.

"How Do I Write?," *Canadian Author and Bookman*, 21 (Dec., 1945), pp. 6-7.

"Canada Between Covers," *Saturday Review of Literature*, 29 (Sept. 7, 1946), pp. 5-6, 28-30.

"Do We Gag Our Writers?," *Maclean's*, 60 (March 1, 1947), pp. 13, 50, 52, 54-55.

"The Future Trend in the Novel," *Canadian Author and Bookman*, 24 (Sept., 1948), pp. 3-5.

"Changing Values in Fiction," *Canadian Author and Bookman*, 25 (1949), pp. 10-18.

"Rhythm in the Novel" [Review], *University of Toronto Quarterly*, 21 (1951-52), pp. 88-90.

"Cape Breton, the Legendary Island," *Saturday Night*, 66 (July 3, 1951), pp. 12-13.

"Fiction in the Age of Science," *Western Humanities Review*, 6 (1952), pp. 325-34.

"My First Book," *Canadian Author and Bookman*, 28 (Summer, 1952), pp. 3-4.

"Canada: The Dramatic North," *Holiday*, 14 (July, 1953), pp. 38-47.

"Storm in Quebec: A National Danger," *Saturday Night*, 69 (May 8, 1954), pp. 7-8.

"Writing in Canada—Its Position Today," *Royal Military College of Canada Review* (1954), pp. 129-35.

"How to Understand French Canada" [Review of *The French Canadians*, by Mason Wade], *Saturday Night*, 70 (March 12, 1955), pp. 9-10.

"The New Nationalism and How It Might Have Looked to Shakespeare," *Maclean's*, 70 (Feb. 16, 1957), pp. 8, 49, 51-52.

"Is Quebec Still the Key to Canadian Politics?," *Saturday Night*, 71 (July 20, 1957), pp. 10-11, 38.

"The People Behind This Peculiar Nation," *The Montrealer*, 32 (December, 1958), pp. 28-31, reprtd. in *Northern Lights*, ed. George E. Nelson (New York, 1960), pp. 513-18.

"La littérature canadienne-française moderne me fait penser à Dickens et à Balzac," *Le Devoir* (November 28, 1959), p. 9.

"The Story of a Novel," *Canadian Literature*, No. 3 (Winter, 1960), pp. 35-39, reprtd. in *Masks of Fiction: Canadian Critics on Canadian Prose*, ed. A.J.M. Smith (Toronto: McClelland and Stewart, 1961), pp. 33-8.

"The Defense of Lady Chatterley," *Canadian Literature*, No. 6 (Autumn, 1960), pp. 18-23.

"Hugh MacLennan's Personal Brief to the Royal Commission on Publications . . . ," *Canadian Library,* 17 (March, 1961), pp. 235-42.

"Postscript on Odysseus," *Canadian Literature*, No. 13 (Summer, 1962), 86-87.

"Reflection on Two Decades," *Canadian Literature*, No. 41 (Summer, 1969), pp. 28-39.

"Two Solitudes that Meet and Greet in Hope and Hate," *Maclean's*, 84 (August, 1971), pp. 19-23, 49-51.

D. FURTHER SELECTED REVIEWS OF MACLENNAN'S NOVELS

Barometer Rising:

Andrew, G.L., Review, *Canadian Forum*, 21 (December, 1941), p. 282.

MacGillivray, J.R., "Fiction," *University of Toronto Quarterly*, 11 (1941-42), pp. 298-300.

Marsh, F.T., Review, *Booklist*, 38 (December 15, 1941), p. 131.

Reading, D., Review, *Library Journal*, 66 (October 1, 1941), p. 841.

Southron, J.S., Review, *New York Times* (October 5, 1941), p. 32.

Two Solitudes:

Anon., "Canadians All," *Commonweal*, 41 (March 16, 1945), p. 546.

Du Bois, William, Review, *New York Times* (January 21, 1945), p. 5.

Kennedy, Leo, Review, *Book Week* (January 21, 1945), p. 1.

Lower, A.R.M., Review, *Canadian Historical Review*, 26 (1945), pp. 326-28.

MacGillivray, J.R., "Fiction," *University of Toronto Quarterly*, 15 (1945-46), pp. 280-83.

McNaught, Eleanor, Review, *Canadian Forum*, 25 (May, 1945), p. 46.

Marchland, L.L., Review, *Booklist*, 41 (March 15, 1945), p. 209.

S., H.L., Review, *Dalhousie Review*, 25 (October, 1945), pp. 378-79.

The Precipice:

Bennett, Virginia, Review, *Commonweal*, 48 (October 1, 1948), p. 601.

Bissell, Claude T., "Fiction" *University of Toronto Quarterly*, 18 (1948-49), pp. 263-65.

Conrad, George, Review, *New York Herald Tribune Weekly Book Review*, (September 12, 1948), p. 5.

Deacon, W.A., "The Literary Scene," *Canadian Author and Bookman*, 25 (Autumn, 1949), p. 36.

Denison, Merrill, Review, *Saturday Review of Literature*, 31 (September 18, 1948), p. 26.

Owen, Patricia, Review, *Canadian Forum*, 28 (November, 1948), p. 190.

Sutcliffe, D., Review, *Christian Science Monitor* (September 23, 1948), p. 15.

Whitmore, Anne, Review, *Library Journal*, 73 (August, 1948), p. 1091.

Each Man's Son:

Allen, Thomas, Review, *New York Times* (April 15, 1951), p. 5.

Ballantyne, M., Review, *Commonweal* 54 (April 20, 1951), p. 46.

Bissell, Claude T., "Fiction," *University of Toronto Quarterly*, 21 (1951-52), pp. 263-64.

Hilton, J., Review, *New York Herald Tribune Weekly Book Review*, (April 8, 1951), p. 6.

Hughes, Riley, Review, *Catholic World*, 173 (July, 1951), p. 311.

Smith, Harrison, "Fate, the Prime Mover," *Saturday Review of Literature*, 34 (June 9, 1951), p. 11.

Snodgrass, E.L., Review, *Christian Century*, 68 (August 1, 1951), p. 895.

Swados, Harvey, Review, *New Republic*, 125 (August 20, 1951), p. 21.

The Watch that Ends the Night:

Biron, Hervé, Review of French translation, *Culture*, 29 (1968), pp. 271-273.

Hicks, Granville, "The Past Recaptured," *Saturday Review*, 42 (February 28, 1959), p. 15.

Hughes, Riley, Review, *Catholic World*, 189 (April, 1959), p. 63.

McPherson, Hugo, Review, *Toronto Daily Star* (February 21, 1959), p. 63.

Mullins, S.G., Review, *Culture*, 20 (1959), p. 360-61.

Ross, Malcolm, Review, *Queen's Quarterly*, 66 (1959), pp. 343-44.

Tallman, W., "An After-glance at MacLennan," *Canadian Literature*, No. 1 (Summer, 1959), pp. 80-81.

Watt, F.W., "Fiction," *University of Toronto Quarterly*, 29 (July, 1960), pp. 460-63.

Woodcock, George, "Odysseus Ever Returning," *Tamarack Review*, No. 11 (Spring, 1959), 77-83.

Return of the Sphinx:

Ader, Dick, Review, *Book World* (November 5, 1967), p. 20.

Buitenhuis, Peter, Review, *New York Times Book Review* (August 20, 1967), p. 4.

Casey, Florence, Review, *Christian Science Monitor* (August 31, 1967), p. 5.

Dalt, G.M., Review, *Tamarack Review*, No. 45 (Autumn, 1967), pp. 114-16.

Fallis, L.S., Review, *Library Journal*, 92 (July, 1967), p. 2606.

McNamara, Eugene, Review, *America*, 117 (September 9, 1967), p. 252.

Maloff, Saul, Review, *Newsweek*, 70 (August 28, 1967), p. 77.

Mauro, Robert, Review, *Saturday Review*, 50 (October 7, 1967), p. 44.

Pickrel, Paul, Review, *Harper's*, 235 (September, 1967), p. 118.

E. FURTHER SELECTED STUDIES OF MACLENNAN

Ballantyne, M.G., "Theology and the Man on the Street: A Catholic Commentary on *Cross-Country*," *Culture*, 10 (December, 1949), pp. 392-96.

Bissell, Claude T., "Introduction," *Two Solitudes, arranged for School Reading* (Toronto: Macmillan, 1951), pp. vii-xxiii.

"The Novel," *The Arts in Canada*, ed. M. Ross (Toronto, 1958).

Bonenfant, Jean-Charles, "Les Livres canadiens-anglais," *La Revue de l'université Laval*, 4 (April, 1950), pp. 742-45.

"Quatres romans récents," *La Revue de l'université Laval*, 6 (September, 1951).

Brown, Alan, "Gabrielle Roy and the Temporary Provincial," *Tamarack Review*, No. 1 (Autumn, 1956), pp. 61-62.

Buitenhuis, Peter, *Hugh MacLennan*, Canadian Writers and their Works (Toronto: Forum House, 1971).

Cockburn, Robert H., *The Novels of Hugh MacLennan* (Montreal: Harvest House, 1971).

Daniells, Roy, "Literature: 1, Poetry and the Novel," *The Culture of Contemporary Canada*, ed. Julian Park (Toronto, 1967), pp. 1-80.

Duncan, Dorothy, "My Author Husband," *Maclean's*, 58 (August 15, 1945), pp. 7, 36, 38, 40.

Eggleston, W., "Thirty and Three," *Queen's Quarterly*, 62 (1955), pp. 264-65.

George, Gerald A., "Theme and Symbol in the Novels of Hugh MacLennan," M. A. thesis (University of Laval, 1967).

Gilley, Robert K., "Myth and Meaning in Three Novels of Hugh MacLennan," M. A. thesis (University of British Columbia, 1967).

Goetsch, Paul, *Das Romanwerk Hugh MacLennans: Eine Studie zum literarischen Nationalismus in Kanada* (Hamburg: Cram, de Gruyter, 1961).
"Too Long to the Courtly Muses—Hugh MacLennan as a Contemporary Writer," *Canadian Literature*, No. 10 (Autumn, 1961), pp. 19-31.

Jones, D. G., *Butterfly on Rock: A Study of Themes and Images in Canadian Literature* (Toronto, 1970).

Kattan, Naim, "Vingt ans après *Deux Solitudes* de Hugh MacLennan," *Le Devoir* (April 25, 1964), p. 13.
"Montreal and French-Canadian Culture: What They Mean to English-Canadian Novelists," *Tamarack Review*, No. 40 (1966), pp. 40-53.
"Le roman canadien anglais," *Lettres nouvelles* (December, 1966—

January, 1967), pp. 21-30.

"Le Visage de Montréal vu par des romanciers de langue anglaise," *Le Devoir* (April 22, 1967), pp. 10-11.

"Le Mystère des deux solitudes," *Le Devoir* (August 26, 1967), p. 13.

"Un Canadien cherche son identité," *Le Devoir* (September 16, 1967), p. 12.

Lucas, Alec, *Hugh MacLennan*, Canadian Writers, 8 (Toronto: McClelland and Stewart, 1970).

Lynn, S., "A Canadian Writer and the Modern World," *Marxist Quarterly*, 1 (Spring, 1962), pp. 36-43.

McPherson, Hugo, "Introduction," *Barometer Rising* (Toronto: McClelland and Stewart, 1958), pp. ix-xv.

"Fiction, 1940-60," *Literary History of Canada*, ed. Carl F. Klinck (Toronto, 1965), pp. 189-98.

Magee, W. H., "Trends in the English-Canadian Novel in the Twentieth Century," Ph. D. thesis (University of Toronto, 1950).

"Trends in the Recent English-Canadian Novel," *Culture*, 10 (March, 1949), pp. 29-42.

Marshall, Tom, "Some Working Notes on *The Watch that Ends the Night*," *Quarry*, 17 (Winter, 1968), pp. 13-16.

Morley, Patricia, "Puritanism in the Novels of Hugh MacLennan," M. A. thesis (Carleton University, 1967).

New, William H., "The Apprenticeship of Discovery," *Canadian Literature*, No. 29 (Summer, 1966), pp. 18-33.

Pacey, Desmond, *Creative Writing in Canada*, rev. ed. (Toronto, 1961), pp. 217-22.

Phelps, Arthur L., "Hugh MacLennan," *Canadian Writers* (Toronto, 1951), pp. 77-84.

Roberts, Ann, "The Dilemma of Hugh MacLennan," *Marxist Quarterly*, 1 (Autumn, 1962), pp. 58-66.

Rubinger, Catherine, "Two Related Solitudes: Canadian Novels in French and English," *Journal of Commonwealth Literature*, No. 3 (July, 1967), pp. 49-57.

Sirois, Antoine, *Montréal dans le roman canadien* (Montreal: Marde Didier, 1970).

Sutherland, Ronald, "Twin Solitudes," *Canadian Literature*, No. 31 (Winter, 1967), pp. 5-24.

"The Fourth Separatism," *Canadian Literature*, No. 45 (Summer, 1970), pp. 7-23 [On *Return of the Sphinx*].

Tallman, W., "Wolf in the Snow," Part One, *Canadian Literature*, No. 5 (Summer, 1960), pp. 7-20 [On *Each Man's Son*].

Thomas, Clare, "Happily Ever After: Canadian Women in Fiction and Fact," *Canadian Literature*, No. 34 (Autumn, 1967), pp. 43-53 [Reference to *Barometer Rising*].

Vallerand, Jean, "Hugh MacLennan, ou la tendresse dans la littérature canadienne," *Le Devoir* (November 28, 1959), p. 11.

Watters, R. E., "Hugh MacLennan and the Canadian Character," *As a Man Thinks...*, ed. E. Morrison and W. Robbins (Toronto, 1953), pp. 228-43.

Weaver, Robert, "A Sociological Approach to Canadian Fiction," *Here and Now*, 1 (June, 1949), pp. 12-15.

Wilson, Edmund, "Hugh MacLennan," *O Canada: An American's Notes on Canadian Culture* (New York, 1965), pp. 59-80.

Wing, Ted, "Puritan Ethic and Social Response in Novels of Sinclair Ross, Robertson Davies, and Hugh MacLennan," M. A. thesis (University of Alberta, 1969).

Woodcock, George, "A Nation's Odyssey: The Novels of Hugh MacLennan," *Canadian Literature*, No. 10 (Autumn, 1961), pp. 7-18, reprtd. in *Odysseus Ever Returning: Essays on Canadian Writers and Writing* (Toronto, 1970), pp. 12-23, and in *Masks of Fiction*, ed. A. J. M. Smith (Toronto, 1961), pp. 128-40.

  Hugh MacLennan, Studies in Canadian Literature (Toronto: Copp Clark, 1969).